HOXTON CHILDHOOD

A. S. Jasper
line drawings by James Boswell

CENTERPRISE PUBLICATIONS
136 KINGSLAND HIGH STREET
LONDON E8

Published by Centerprise
in association with John Bunting Ltd
136 Kingsland High Street, London E8
© 1969 A S Jasper
Printed in Great Britain
by Expression Printers Ltd, 5 Kingsbury Road, N1
Reprinted 1974, 1975
ISBN 0 903738 02 3

To My Mother
and to all the mothers of that time

Author's Father 1922   Author's Mother 1922

Author 1922

INTRODUCTION

For this new edition of A. S. Jaspar's widely acclaimed autobiography, we thought it appropriate to describe some of the effects of Mr Jaspar's book in the locality, and to outline further developments in the bringing of other local writing to the attention of a wider audience.

'A Hoxton Childhood' was originally serialised in the monthly magazine of the Hackney Library Service, Profile. Interest in these reminiscences was so great that the commercial publishers, Barrie & Jenkins then issued the autobiography complete with considerable success. One of the most gratifying aspects of its publication was the confidence it gave to many other people in the East End to think about writing about their own lives as well, lives which at first sight may have seemed 'unimportant' but when described conveyed great depth and richness.

Two years ago the Hackney Workers' Educational Association began a project called, 'A Peoples' Autobiography of Hackney', which consisted of a group of local people who met regularly and spent many evenings tape-recording the reminiscences of elderly people in the borough. The Library Service was obviously interested in these tapes as archive material and made a small contribution to the project's costs. Since then cooperation between the two bodies has grown to the extent that we have now entered on a co-operative publishing venture to bring into being a number of other publications of local interest. Many of these proposed publications have arisen from the tapes, and two of them have already been published: 'When I was a Child' by Dot Starn, and 'Years of Change' by Arthur Newton. Shortly to follow are the autobiography of a local taxi-driver, 'Licence to Live' by Ron Barnes, and a collection of anecdotes about Doctor Jelley, 'The Threepenny Doctor', taken from sixteen taped interviews with local elderly people.

Also of note is the reception of these publications by local schools. 'A Hoxton Childhood' is now widely read in secondary schools, together with the other publications and many children have been able, perhaps for the first time, to begin to understand the historical significance of their own parents' and grandparents' lives. Mention must also be made of the Centerprise Bookshop which has been very helpful in providing an efficient means of distributing these publications, as well as providing other facilities for their production.

We hope that these publications, and their successors, will provide a nostalgic but realistic picture of the past of this interesting East End Borough as seen through the lives of some of its residents who participated fully in the past they describe.

Cllr Bob Masters
Chairman, Hackney Libraries & Amenities Committee

Ken Worpole
Secretary, Hackney Workers' Educational Association

Chapter One

'I ALWAYS told you he's no bleeding good and nothing good will come of it if they get married.' Those were my father's words after discovering my sister Mary was four months pregnant. This knowledge came to my parents' notice due to the following circumstances.

One Sunday evening my mother and father had gone for their Sunday night drink—my eldest sister Mary was with Gerry her boy-friend. My older brother Bert was out scrounging with his friends somewhere in Hoxton, and my second eldest sister Jo' was also out with friends. My baby sister Molly was with Mother and Father outside the pub in a pram. This left me with Mary and Gerry alone in the house. I suddenly heard Mary and Gerry having a terrific row, and Gerry slammed out of the house. Mary was crying her eyes out. She was still crying when she called me to the kitchen. 'Jan, would you go to the chemist for me?' I asked her what I had to get, and she gave me a blue bottle and asked me to get 'twopennyworth of spirits of salts'. I was only about eight years old at the time and didn't know the difference between spirits of salts or medicine of any sort.

In those days, 1913, a chemist was open in Hoxton until late on Sunday nights. Off I went. At that time we were living in Canal Road, and I only had to walk into Hyde Road then I was in the Hoxton market. To get to the chemist I had to pass the Kings Arms public house; this was situated in the narrow way of Hoxton. As I passed, I saw my mother standing in the passageway of the pub. 'Whatever are you doing out this time of the night?' says my mother. I had to tell her where I was going and what I had to get. When she heard my story she was livid. 'Give me that bloody bottle,' and there was a crash as she slung it in the road.

My father was having a drink in the bar with his pal. 'Bill,' Mum calls out. 'I want you a minute.' Out comes Dad. My mother explains why I am there, and they decide to go home and see what it's all about.

On arriving home they found Mary lying on her bed, still crying. My mother eventually got the story from her. It seemed Gerry had a rough home life and some months previous Mum had let him have a room, but it looked as if he spent more time in my sister's room than he did in his own. My father always reckoned Gerry was a small-time crook. His reason being Gerry would depart from the house about 4 a.m. and come home at all times during the day. When the old man asked him why he kept such erratic hours, Gerry's answer was that he worked in the fish market.

Anyhow, to get back to the beginning. It was decided that whatever Gerry's failings he would have to marry my sister Mary. Gerry never came back that night so it was decided to wait until next day to work things out.

Before going on with the story I think I should give a

description of my family. My father was about forty years of age at the time: he had a distinct Roman nose, a full moustache, slightly bandy legs and drooping shoulders. His main object in life was to be continually drunk, and he had every opportunity to keep that way. His job was delivering overmantels and small furniture to various places in East London. He used to go out at five in the morning. First call was the local pub for rum and milk; this he could keep up all day. He always had money: of every three articles he delivered, one was nicked, and the proceeds shared among the men who loaded him up. But at home he was tight with his money. I don't ever remember my mother having a week's wages off him—six or seven shillings was the most she ever received.

The reason he never gave her regular wages was he knew my mother could always earn a few shillings with her machine. To me, my mother was the most wonderful woman on earth. I find it hard to describe the love that she gave us. She had come to this country at the age of eighteen. Her family were musicians and had played at the royal Dutch Court. I never discovered why they emigrated—probably thought they could do better here. When I was old enough to understand, I asked her what made her marry a man like my father. She told me that he had taken her out many times, but she always had to be home early for my grandmother was very strict. Eventually one night he brought her home past midnight and Grandmother refused to open the door. Consequently, he took her to his own place, made her pregnant and they had to get married. He deceived her from the start: she never got over the fact that he gave her a brass wedding ring.

At the time this story starts she had had six children and she loved every one of us. My eldest brother Will I never knew much about—he joined the Navy at fifteen and a half.

My eldest sister Mary, like all working girls at that time, went to work in a factory and went out at nights. She was small in build, not awfully good looking, and dressed better than most girls because Mum always made her dresses and skirts. My brother Bert was a roamer and a local tough. I don't remember much of him at the time. He was about fifteen, and he was always out. Mum was so afraid of the company he kept that she had him put on a training ship at fifteen and a half. It definitely kept him from going crooked.

My second sister Jo' was very different. Since my earliest memories I was always with her. She would take me to school, and would come for me at four and I was allowed to sit next to her in class until four-thirty. She was very good looking and had fair wavy hair. She was always at my mother's call and for years was her right hand in helping in the house and helping sell the articles of clothing Mum made.

I was about eight years old at the time and rather a big boy for my age. My sisters used to make a fuss of me and my mother would hardly let me out of her sight. I dearly loved my mother, and now at sixty years of age her memory and love are still with me.

This leaves us with the baby of the family, Molly, three years old, very pretty with golden curls. I well remember the day she was born.

We were living then at number three Clinger Street,

Hoxton, in a hovel on the ground floor. It comprised two rooms and a kitchen, with an outside lavatory which also served the family upstairs. I was five years old. My mother and father and myself slept in the front room. My sister Mary was fifteen and my sister Jo' was eleven. They slept in the back room in one iron bedstead, with brother Bert who was thirteen in the same room. Being only a small child, I used to sleep against the wall, next to my mother in my parents' bed. In the summer we lived in the kitchen, which had a stone floor, an old iron cooking range and was very dark. In the winter it was very cold and damp so we lived in the front room where my mother and father slept. For lighting we had gas brackets with 'fish tail' burners. It was a terrible crush when we were all home having our meals in the bedroom.

August 17th, 1910, was a very hot day. About eleven o'clock that morning my sister Jo' was told to take me out and play in the playground, which was situated somewhere at the back of Hammond Square School. I remember seeing a lot of activity going on in the house that morning. The lady upstairs was doing a lot of running around and I also remember seeing a nurse arrive with a black Gladstone bag. My sister kept me out until she thought it was time for dinner—not that we ever had much. When we arrived home, she told me to wait outside and she would come and tell me when it was all right for me to come in.

A few moments later she came out for me. 'Come and have a look at what Mum has bought you.' As I entered the door I could hear a baby crying. My little sister Molly had been born while I was out playing. My eyes must have opened wide in wonderment as I was lifted up to see the new baby. My mother told my sister Jo' to lay me next to her, as I started to cry. My mother cuddled me up close to her in her efforts to stop me crying. She had always made such a fuss of me, and I suppose I must have realised my nose had been put out of joint. I never left my mother all that day. My sister got the room tidied up and my grandmother came. My sister was sent to the Kings Arms, a public house my father used in Hoxton, about eight o'clock that night to tell him to come home as Mum had been 'confined'. He eventually came home more drunk than sober. I hardly ever remember him being sober. He didn't seem to show much interest in the baby and after a while went out again.

Came time for going to bed. My mother told me I would have to sleep with my sister Jo' as I was now getting a 'big boy'. Also, I could not sleep with her in the big bed because of the baby. I cried and cried my eyes out. It was understood. I had never known anything else. I had always slept in my parents' bed. In the end, I must have been pacified and went with my sister Jo'. She laid me in her bed and quickly got in beside me and tried to cuddle me off to sleep. I must have gone to bed sobbing my heart out at leaving my mother. In the room was a small paraffin lamp. They were bought for a penny. I remember waking up in the night and seeing the shadows that were cast by the lamp as the flame moved. I cried out in fright. Everyone woke up, including my parents. My father was swearing and shouting, 'Keep that bloody kid quiet can't yer.' In the end, my mother shouted through the thin walls to 'Bring him in here'. My sister carried me in and my father was still in a rage, swearing and shouting in his half-drunken stupor. My mother placed a pillow at the foot of the bed, and laid me down to sleep. Feeling her next to me, I soon went off.

Next morning I was dressed and taken out again to play because the nurse was coming. After she had been I went in to my mother and refused to leave her. I also wanted to be with my new sister. Twelve o'clock came and my father came in. 'What brings you home at this time of day?' my mother asked. He had never been known to come home at midday, hence my mother's question. He explained that his mates at work had collected a few shillings for a colleague whose baby had just died, and was being buried that afternoon. He had to take it to Wilmer Gardens where the chap lived. My mother asked him to take me with him as the lady upstairs was coming down to clean up. Reluctantly, he took me with him. I had not the slightest idea what it was all about. He held me by the hand and took me to a block of broken-down tenement dwellings at the top left-hand side of Wilmer Gardens.

They were directly opposite North's Lodging House. These tenements were set back well away from the road and they were rat-infested. To get to the front entrance, one had to cross a vast square of waste ground. In the summer, this was just a dust and rubbish heap. In the winter, it was a sea of mud and filth. The front doors of the tenements, or what was left of them, were always open. Dirty and half-starved children were playing in the filth and garbage that had collected outside. To get to the flat of my father's workmate we had to climb a flight of rickety stairs. As we passed the other flats on our way up, I could smell the nauseating odours that came from the rooms. I could hear some of the occupants swearing and rowing and children crying.

We eventually reached our destination, and were told to come in the open door. I still remember my father's friend telling him how his little son had died. It could have only been a few weeks old. His eyes were red with crying. The remaining children were sitting around a wooden table with newspaper for a tablecloth. After my father gave him the few shillings he had collected, he was asked if he would like to see the baby before the undertaker arrived to screw down the coffin. I believe it was the thing everyone did in those days. My father said he would and told me to stay put. This I would not do. I held on to his hand and insisted on going with him. After giving me a scolding, he told me I could come with him.

On an old chest-of-drawers in a room with three beds in was a little white coffin. My father's friend slid back the lid and amid tears said to my father, 'What about him, Bill?' meaning me. My father replied, 'He's all right,' and beckoning to me, said, 'Come and have a look, boy.' He lifted me up to see the dead baby. I have never forgotten that face. In my tiny childish mind, I got my first glimpse of peace.

But to get back to the story of Mary and Gerry—on the Monday Gerry was sent for, my father's instructions were: 'If he don't come I'll bleeding well come and get him.' I think my brother Bert went with the message on the Monday night. Gerry arrived. He was a short corpulent chap, thin fair hair, heavy jowls on his face, thought the world of himself, and was prepared for a fight with my father. Although my sister had been courting him for some time, he had never been in our company much. On the two or three times he had been with us he never left a very good impression. After a terrific argument and several threats by Gerry and my father to punch each other's heads in, it was decided that the wedding would take place. First, where were they going to live? They couldn't live with us—we already had a couple with three children upstairs. It was agreed that Mother would try to find a bigger house.

In those days it was easy; one only had to go to an agent, pay the first week's rent and move in. On more than one occasion my father came home late, drunk as usual, and was told by the next-door neighbours we 'didn't live there any more'. We had owed so much rent that the agent had threatened to throw us in the road if we didn't pay up.

On this occasion it wasn't that we owed so much rent but the fact we had to have a larger house. My mother duly found and inspected a house in Salisbury Street, New North Road. It wasn't a bad area and I always remember it was the nicest house we ever had.

Mary said she would like the top front room. Gerry agreed it would be fine and it was duly decided to take it. My father wasn't consulted on moving. It hardly mattered to him where he lived, he was hardly ever in: so long as a pub was near he didn't care. The moving was to take place on the following Saturday afternoon. My brother Bert was detailed to 'go and get a barrow' on the Saturday morning. This was got from a local costermongers. A deposit of two shillings was required and the barrow was ours for the day. If we returned it before nine at night we were given one and sixpence back.

After dinner on the Saturday the move started. Gerry hadn't arrived after promising to be there early. My mother supervised the packing and tying up of the bedding. It must have been a good twenty minutes walk from Canal Road to Salisbury Street, so one can guess the amount of journeys that had to be done. Loads were packed and tied on that barrow that only Eastern labourers would attempt to move. Midway through moving, Gerry arrived. 'What time do you call this?' my mother asked him. His reply was, 'I had to work late in the fish market.' Gerry could just not tell the truth. It was discovered afterwards that a neighbour had seen him playing pitch-and-toss in a gambling school in Wilmer Gardens. Wilmer Gardens was a notorious place for local villains and petty criminals. It boasted of a lodging house which housed them; often after a crime in Hoxton, the police would turn the inmates out to see if the suspects were there.

Gerry did his share of pulling the barrow and we eventually finished about 9.30 p.m. Mary and Jo' got cracking on putting up the beds and undoing bundles. Gerry helped, but tried every now and then to snatch a quick snog with Mary. In the end he gave up: too many of us were running all over the house putting things in various rooms.

About eleven it was decided we had had enough. My mother made cocoa and cut bread and butter which we set into with gusto; having had nothing to eat since dinner-time, we were all ravenously hungry. Gerry was asked to stay but declined. Since the discovery of my sister's pregnancy he was not on very good terms with my father. Whenever they met, they eyed each other like two punch-drunk boxers waiting for the first blow to fall. My mother's patience somehow seemed to delay any fighting tactics. Anyhow, Gerry promised to come Sunday to tea.

Sunday morning we all got up early and put the house in ship-shape order. Before dinner I was instructed to go to Pimlico Walk which is the top end of Hoxton. This was an alley-way, next to the old Britannia Theatre. One could buy almost anything in the Walk on Sunday. I had to get a pint of winkles and a pennyworth of watercress. This constituted the main item for Sunday tea. Usually the old man would come in drunk, have his dinner and then go and sleep it off until tea-time. Woe-betide the peace of the household if there was no winkles and watercress. I've seen him create something awful. He would come downstairs, sit down at the table and say, 'No cress; you know bloody well I always have them.' Then the trouble would start: we kids were always terrified and immediately went to our mother's side. She would stand so much from him that in the end her patience was exhausted. Mum was quiet and would try by all means to talk him down. When this failed, she would go berserk and clump the old man for all she was worth. I've seen her rip the shirt off his back; he'd finish up with just the collarband round his neck.

But to get back to the occasion of the first Sunday tea in the new house. Everything went very smoothly during tea. Gerry ate as though he had eaten nothing for weeks. The old man asked Gerry what his job in the fish market was. 'Portering,' said Gerry. 'Why don't you bring home a bit of fish now and then?' said the old man. 'I can always do that, Bill,' says Gerry, who was now trying to be good friends by calling my father by his Christian name. 'I'll drop some in as I knock off tomorrow.' After tea the old man gets ready for his visit to the local pub; at seven o'clock he was off. Gerry entertained the family with a few card tricks; he certainly could manipulate the cards. About nine o'clock my mother suggested plans should be worked out for the forthcoming wedding as time was getting near. It was agreed that the next day, after work, Mary and Gerry would go and put the banns up. My sisters were beginning to get a little excited at the prospect of the wedding. After all, Mary was the first one in the family to get wed and Mum was sure to see only the best was good enough. So there the discussion ended and we were all looking forward to the excitement and preparation in the forthcoming weeks.

Monday afternoon Gerry came round on a bike. 'Here you are, Ma,' he says, and gave Mum four big herrings wrapped in newspaper. 'Thanks, Gerry,' says Mum. 'They're straight from the market, Ma, so they're nice and fresh.' Mum made him a cup of tea and asked him where he got his bicycle from. Since he had been calling in of late we noticed on two or three occasions he had a different bike. 'I managed to pick it up cheap, Ma, and hope to do it up, sell it and make a few bob,' Gerry replied. If Mum was suspicious she kept it to herself. I remember this all so well because I was not at school; we had not had time to get me initiated at a local school since moving.

Towards seven o'clock that night my father came home and wanted to know what arrangements had been made for the wedding. 'I still don't think he's any cop and cannot see any good coming of this,' says the old man. He'd had a few beers or rums and was in his usual aggressive mood. 'Don't talk that way,' said Mum, 'he's not a bad chap and he does work in the fish market. Just look what he brought home today.' Mum gets the four herrings from the larder and shows him. The old man picked up a herring, looked at it in disgust, and with, 'He don't bleeding well fool me, mate,' slung it back on the plate. 'He don't work in no bloody fish market. Probably bought them on a stall in Hoxton to make it look good.'

Mum started to cook the herrings and I noticed the old man didn't refuse his one. But he never altered his mind about Gerry. He treated him with suspicion, and always would.

The three weeks ahead were looked forward to with excitement and anticipation. First, the house had to be decorated; my mother and sister set into this with gusto. Wallpaper was about threepence a roll; a ball of whitening and boiled size made the whitewash for the ceiling. Gerry did his own room up. This he called the 'Bridal Suite'. When they had finished it looked very nice. Of all the houses we ever lived in (and we lived in plenty) this was the nicest and most homely place in my memory. Upstairs in the front was a large bedroom, Mary's and Gerry's. At the back, another bedroom which my mother and father used. On the right-hand side was a fantastically large room which went from front to back of the house. It was over a stable. This the children used. A curtain divided the room in two halves, one half for my sisters and the other for my brother and myself. Four iron bedsteads and an old dressing-table were the furnishings. Downstairs was a front room (parlour if one had anything to put in it), at the rear a living-room with kitchen range and a washhouse adjoining. A small garden added to our pleasure. All this and rates paid for eight shillings a week.

After decorating, Gerry said he would like to keep fowls. My mother offered no resistance to this, but the old man, as usual, got his back up at the thought. Gerry got over this by offering to take him out for a drink at the Bridport Arms—this was the local pub, only at the end of the street and very convenient for the old man. On their return, permission was duly granted and next day Gerry built his chicken-house. I must say he made it very attractive; he whitewashed the inside and painted the outside green. It was so nice that I as a child envied the chickens. On the Sunday, I went with Gerry down Petticoat Lane to see what was going cheap in the chicken line. After inspecting every stall, we finished up with one hen which, after a lot of bargaining, Gerry got for four shillings. Under Gerry's arm went the hen and we safely got it home. The first day home it laid an egg. I shall never forget the look on

Gerry's face. For months after, it was his pride and joy.

A conference was called which consisted of Mum, my sisters and Gerry's mother and father, in order to make arrangements for the coming wedding which was not far off now. It was the first time we had met Gerry's parents. His mother was a large woman with a thin face and her hair tied up in a knot at the back. She had had a very hard life. Her first husband had died when her four children were very young. When the oldest was about fourteen years she married again. Her husband was Gerry's stepfather. It seemed he was cruel to the children and ill-treated his wife. Consequently, when they were old enough to go to work they left home one after the other.

Gerry's stepfather was a huge man. A fish fryer by trade, he carried the scars of his job all over his arms. They were one mass of scars due to burning oil splashes. His face was horrible. My sister Jo' called him Battered Face (she usually had a nickname for everyone). His face seemed all bashed in. This, Gerry told us, was caused by fighting and brawling in his younger days. His right eye looked natural, but the left was glazed, and looked like an eye without a pupil. I never got near him. He used to terrify me.

Anyhow, it was agreed that they would come to the wedding and would help where they could with food, crockery, glasses and all things that were needed. What about music? They had a gramophone and records. The latest model with disc records. This was out of the blue. We only had a phonograph with 'cylinder' records. We gratefully accepted the loan of the gramophone. 'Could anyone play a mouth organ?' 'Yes,' we said. My eldest brother was coming home on leave from the Navy for the wedding, and he was an expert. Now we were all set for the great day regarding music. After the conference ended, Battered Face invited all to a drink at the Bridport. All parted good friends and they arranged to see us all on Sunday fortnight at 9.30 a.m.

The next two weeks were a hard time for my mother. She was trying to give a good show for my sister but lacked the necessary cash to do all she would have liked. One day, she called my father in the front room and said, 'Bill, I'd like an overmantel in here, how much can you get one for?' He could have got one for nothing. As I have already explained, his job was delivering these things and being in a swindle at work, with his two mates, there was no question of paying. He said he could not get one 'under twenty-five shillings' and he must have the cash first, otherwise 'no deal'. Mum paid him and, as time went on, got rather worried when no overmantel showed up. Two days before the wedding she threatened to 'brain him' if it did not show up in time. He delivered it next day. He knew her threat would be carried out.

The wedding date was also near my birthday. I had been promised a watch if I would continue to be a 'good boy'. In Bridport Place there was a pawnshop by the name of Long & Doughty. If one took goods there to pawn, the local saying was, 'A long time in and doubt if they ever come out.' In those days nearly everyone had to go to 'Pawn'. One day, Mum wanted a few bob and took a parcel of clothes or bedsheets. It was fascinating to see the procedure. One went into a cubicle where the gent behind the counter usually knew his customers. 'How much?' were his first words. 'Ten shillings,' says Mum. 'Seven,' says the gent behind the counter. 'Oh Christ,' says Mum, 'don't be like that, Sid.' 'All right,' says Sid, 'I'll make it eight bob, but don't forget it's the last time I take this lot in.' Mum had to settle for eight bob and Sid would then proceed as follows. He would pin the parcel up for storage with a very thick pin, then write out the ticket. Three tickets were needed. One to pin on the parcel, one for the record and one for the customer. The mechanism of the pen had to be seen to be believed. There were three inkwells for the three wire nibs, all controlled by the penholder. Sid would then proceed to write the tickets by picking up the penholder, dipping the three nibs in the three inkwells and then writing as though one ticket. One halfpenny was deducted from the loan for the ticket. On Saturday, if the parcel was required, I would be sent to Long & Doughty to redeem it. First, one handed in the ticket. This was placed in a small bag and hauled up by a piece of rope by whoever was working upstairs. When the parcel was found, it would come down the hatch with a crash. Sid would call out the name on the ticket and I would shout out 'One' or 'Two' according to the number of parcels there were. On redemption, the interest charge was one halfpenny per two shillings per month.

To get back to my watch I was going to have for my birthday. Coming out of the pawnshop, I saw a silver pocket watch marked up for four and ninepence. I told Mum I would like one just like that. She was a good sort and suggested we go in and have a look. This we did and not having the cash to spare, Sid behind the counter suggested we 'pay off' and get it when we paid the balance. Mum paid a shilling deposit and promised me I would have it in time for the wedding. Mum kept her promise. I got the watch a day before Mary's wedding. What happened to it I will tell later.

It was decided that my brother Bert and I were to have new suits. Bert was never worried about clothes. One of his objects in life was swimming. This he would do in the local canal every night in the summer. Crowds used to gather to watch the boys perform, and Bert would dive off the bridge for a ha'penny or off 'the Pipe'—a waste-water duct that was higher—for a penny. He was always coming home with some of his clothes missing. It was either a shirt or his boots. While the lads were swimming, the rogues would go round the heaps of clothes and help themselves. I always remember one night in particular. It got very late and Bert hadn't arrived home. Near midnight he crept in without his trousers. He had to wait until it was dark and the streets deserted before he could venture home. Consequently, Mum was never worried too much regarding his clothes. Anyhow, a local tally-man was contacted and Bert and I had a new suit. I am sure it was the first new suit he ever had in his life. My sisters were more fortunate. Mum could always make them their dresses. They also worked very hard getting the place in order, and Gerry continued to call in at all times. But he always had a different bike, 'one he had bought cheap and was going to do up' he would say.

We now come to the day before the wedding. We

were all getting excited, and a feeling of jollity was in the air. My eldest brother came home on leave from the Navy and was going to be best man. He was a tall, good-looking chap, and well he knew it. He immediately took a firm dislike to Gerry. Why, I don't know. Gerry was a rough diamond, but apart from the mystery surrounding the way he got his living, I could never see any reason to dislike him. The house was all in order and prepared for the next day's celebration. Being Saturday night, all retired to the Bridport Arms for a pre-celebration drink. Towards closing time the trouble started. My father, brother, Gerry and several friends were drinking up; Gerry was well away. He was also well aware of my brother's feelings towards him. The old man's feeling of animosity towards Gerry was sunk with the rum and beer he was drinking. 'Come on, Gerry, drink up,' my father said. 'Watch it, Dad, he's only a boy,' replied my brother. That did it. Gerry immediately got his back up. 'Who are you calling a boy? I'm old enough to give you a bleeding good hiding,' and right away a fight started. Fists and pints were flying all over the place. Gerry really got stuck in. Someone ran home to my mother and sisters to tell them what was happening. They all went in the pub, managed to get order restored and finally coaxed them to come home. Mum told them they should be ashamed of themselves. For bridegroom and best man to fight the night before the wedding was terrible. Mum had two arms that were like large legs of mutton and when they saw her begin to roll her sleeves up they knew it was time to call a halt. Friendship was restored by opening up one of the several gallon jars of ale that had been got in for the wedding. All wished each other the best of luck and all ended well. Brother Will shook hands with Gerry before he left and promised he wouldn't be late in the morning. They parted the best of pals.

There wasn't much sleep that night. Very early in the morning my sisters got up and made tea and started preparing for the great day. The wedding was at 10 a.m. This did not leave a lot of time for formalities. It was a walking wedding. Ten minutes to the church. After tea and toast, the old man came downstairs, still half dazed by the beer and the fight the night before. He didn't want anything to eat and so got stuck into a rum and milk and wanted to know 'how much bleeding longer he would have to wait' for the lavatory to be available. Mum dressed my young sister and myself and gave us strict instructions to 'keep ourselves clean' and for me to look after Molly. The old man started to get himself ready; he'd bought himself a pair of striped trousers and a bobtail coat, all second-hand from the stall in Hoxton market. My sisters just could not keep a straight face. I thought they were going in hysterics when he started to put on a collar and tie; he had never worn one in his life. They eventually got it on for him after a lot of swearing and blinding. The coat was going green with age. He did look a sight, with brown boots, striped trousers, a semi-green bobtail coat and a flat cap. But he was quite pleased with himself. What was good enough for the gentry was good enough for him, he insisted. My brother Bert looked a different boy; I had never seen him look so smart. My sisters looked good too. Jo' was dressed in a nice white blouse with a sailor collar and a white 'Jabot' in the front. Her hair was nice and wavy and she looked good. Mary was similarly dressed. It was the fashion in those days to wear 'skirt and blouse' for most occasions. She looked very nice. Mum looked nice too. I'll always remember her blue blouse trimmed with lace and a large cameo brooch.

My brother Will went off to meet Gerry while we all set off walking to the church. Being early on a Sunday morning there was hardly anyone about. We must have looked a sight as we walked along the street, especially the old man. My sisters were taking the mickey out of him all the way, but were careful not to let him notice. We arrived in church and took our places. Gerry's mother and father arrived and several invited friends. My brother and Gerry were late arrivals. I can see Gerry to this day walking to the altar. I think everyone gasped for breath as he walked up the aisle. He had Bulldog-toe shoes, peg-top trousers, a silk sash round his stomach, white shirt, no collar, a large silk scarf tied in a double knot around his neck, with the ends tucked in his braces, a long coat with turnback cuffs and pearl buttons and a flat cap like a pancake. All local 'boys' dressed like that in those days.

The marriage ceremony was duly performed. While Gerry and Mary were in the vestry, we all waited outside the church ready to pelt them with confetti. We then started to walk home. We were quite a crowd by now and if we looked a sight going, goodness knows what we looked like coming back. Mary was in front holding Gerry's arm. Gerry had his hands in his pockets, his long coat flapping from side to side with each step he took. The old man had had a few rums before leaving home and was well away in his bobtail with a large red handkerchief hanging out of the tail pocket. It didn't take us long to get home. I think my mother and my sister Jo' were a little embarrassed by the antics of the two nifty dressers and hurried them as quickly out of sight as they could. Mum and my sisters had set the wedding breakfast before going to church and it didn't take us long to get stuck in. Everyone was drinking and good luck was wished by all to the bride and groom. After breakfast, all were set for a good time. Mum and my sisters cleared away and started to prepare dinner. A leg of pork went in the oven with two chickens. Never in our natural lives had we known such times.

I was very happy; my watch was keeping good time and I suppose I was looking at it every five minutes. While dinner was being prepared my father suggested all the men retire to the front room for a 'wet', it being too early to go to the Bridport Arms. Their conversation was of a sporting nature. Boxers of the day were discussed. Bombardier Billy Wells, Jack Johnson, Tancy Lee and lots more. Prospects of the forthcoming Derby were also considered. Gerry reckoned he had a cert which was an outsider, much to the old man's disgust, who said the favourite just 'could not lose'. On the Saturday before the wedding several gallons of ale and bottles of spirits had been ordered and delivered, and the old man suggested that this was the time to have a 'whip round' to pay for it. Everyone paid their share, and it was agreed that all would go to the Bridport to pay the bill as soon as they opened at twelve-thirty. It would also be a good opportunity to have a few before dinner. At twelve-thirty prompt, all male members were away. At one-thirty Gerry came back to the house and suggested all the females 'come up for a drink'. Gerry was getting well oiled and in a very happy mood. My young sister and I were standing at the front door as they all went out, when Gerry asked us if we would like an 'ice cream'. He gave me fourpence to get two ices. Gerry had never given me fourpence all the time we had known him and I was beginning to hope the wedding would last for ever.

While everyone was up at the Bridport, my brother Bert was alone in the house with all the gallon jars of ale. He must have thought 'what was good enough for the grown-ups was good enough for him'. He decided to try a half pint. Eventually he decided to try another, and by the time Mum and all the females returned he was blind-drunk. He was in a terrible state. Gerry's ma picked him up and laid him out in the garden and gave him soda-water to try and make him sick. It was decided to leave him there and let him sleep it off.

Dinner was ready to serve out, but the males were not home yet. I was detailed to go up the pub and ask them to come home. I managed to get my brother's eye and told them dinner was ready, would they come home immediately. If not, Mum was coming up herself to have them out. As soon as I mentioned 'Mum was coming', for the sake of peace they decided to come home. How they all managed to sit round the table, I'll never know. Nothing was impossible to my mother. During dinner several people asked where Bert was. After Mum had explained what had happened, they all agreed it was best to leave him to try and sleep it off.

Everyone praised Mum for the dinner and all said it was the best they had ever had. My sisters started to clear away and several of the men wanted to go to the lavatory pretty urgently. The first one out was Gerry's stepfather. On trying to open the door, he found it was locked from the inside. He bashed on the door and roared, 'How long?' It seemed during dinner my brother Bert had recovered enough to go to the lavatory and feeling sick and bad had locked himself in and was out to the wide. My father and several others came out to see what all the shouting was about. Gerry started to bang on the door and shouted, 'Hurry up, Bert, my father want to go.' 'Sod off,' says Bert, 'I feel sick.' By now Gerry's stepfather was raving and threatened to 'bash the bleeding door in'. 'Go to your house and use your own closet,' says Bert. 'Ain't it all right,' says Gerry's stepfather. 'I'm expected to go all the bleedin' way to London Fields to use the soddin' lavvo.' 'We've got to get him out somehow,' says Gerry. Eventually Mum arrived on the scene and somehow coaxed him 'to be reasonable'. She managed to get him to slide the bolt and when he emerged it was a sight for sore eyes. He'd had diarrhoea very badly and was sick all over his new suit. 'That's the last bloody suit you'll ever get from me,' declared Mum. She was terribly annoyed. Mary and Jo' managed to get him inside and cleaned him up.

After that rumpus over the lavatory, things settled down to normal. Everyone was tired and it was decided that all the older guests should try to get some sleep in preparation for the party that night. I can't remember what became of Gerry and Mary—probably locked themselves in their 'Bridal Suite' as he called it. I remember my father going to his own bed. As he took his trousers off, his money fell out of his pocket. He was so drunk he couldn't bend down to find it. I was going upstairs as this happened and looked in the door and saw some cash on the floor. Knowing he always kept Mum short, I dived under the bed and picked up a two-shilling piece. He didn't know it was me, but in his stupor he knew someone was there and threatened to 'bash their bleeding brains out if he caught them'. I slid out, found Mum and gave her the two shillings I managed to pick up. She asked me how I came by it, and I explained what had happened. 'Good boy,' she says, and upstairs she went. Dad was now out to the world, so she had all the silver and left him the coppers. When he woke up he never made any reference to his loss. Gerry's mother and father and several others went into our big bedroom to try and sleep. There was a lot of laughing and joking going on. Gerry's ma was telling his father 'not to try and take bleeding liberties with her' and to 'wait till he got to his own place'. After a while everyone seemed to doze off and all was quiet.

About five-thirty, Mum decided it was time to get tea ready. Nobody seemed to want much. The old man had his winkles and cress and was fighting fit. After tea everyone retired to the front room and the drinks were soon flowing. Jo' put the records on. We had the top hits of the day. 'See them Shuffling Along', 'Alexander's Ragtime Band', we had the lot. My eldest brother's mate arrived and he immediately took up with my sister Jo'. They got the dancing going and everything was soon under way. Mum liked a waltz, and one of the male guests named George also liked to waltz. He was a nice-looking chap and he could dance. He took to Mum and they had several dances together. After a while someone suggested a song. First to go was Gerry's stepfather. His song was, 'I've fought and bled for England but what has she done for me?' This was all about a soldier returned from the wars crippled and unable to work and was reduced to begging in the streets. 'Battered Face' sang in a voice that nearly busted all the looking-glasses in the new overmantel. All agreed it was 'bleedin' well sung' and he was invited to 'drink up'.

Meantime, I was still admiring my watch and thought how lucky I was to own such a masterpiece. My father had somehow managed to borrow an accordion. He always boasted he could play. All he could do was vamp on two notes. Anyhow, he did his stuff with a song called 'They're all very fine and large, some are fat and prime'. This was a ditty about a chap who goes to a common lodging house for a night's 'kip' and comes out next morning running alive'o. The old man did all the actions like scratching himself and it went down well. Everyone said, 'Well done, Bill. What about another one?' He was only too happy to oblige with 'Across the Bridge at Midnight', accompanied by my brother on the mouth organ. This was a song about a gambler who had lost all his money at cards and thought about throwing himself in the river. The old man would have gone on for ever but he got shouted down as the younger ones wanted the gramophone. Dancing started again and George suggested another waltz to Mum who was pleased to accept. By this time the old man was well out and was beginning to take a dim view of Mum dancing with George all night. When they had finished their dance, he sat down next to Mum and started nagging. She stuck it for as long as she possibly could and then suddenly picked up the shovel in the hearth and clouted him round the face. She called him all the 'miserable old gits' she could lay her tongue to. This started a real bust-up.

Everyone was on Mum's side and all agreed there was 'no harm in it'; George was prepared to settle it out in the road with the old man, which he readily agreed to. But he was dead crafty. To get out to the street he had to pass the stairs. As he reached them he shot up halfway, grabbed the banisters with one hand and offered to 'challenge' anyone who came near him. He was in a commanding position to lash out with one fist and one boot. Mary was crying her eyes out. To think that the 'ole sod' should start a fight on her wedding day. Gerry's stepfather, who could have broken our old man in half, somehow got order and led him back to the front room. He gave him a drink and made him promise to behave himself. Soon everything seemed forgotten and everyone was drinking up again and dancing, but Mum and the old man were sitting glaring at each other and we were all afraid another fight was going to start again.

I sat on Mum's knee and showed her my treasured watch. Mary and Jo' cut loads of sandwiches which were offered round with mustard pickles, pickled onions and gherkins. This seemed to quieten everyone down. After the sandwiches Mary and Jo' sang their duet, 'When we went to school together', with mouth organ accompaniment which was well received. The old man wanted to play the accordion again, but was promptly told to 'put the bloody thing down'. He had no alternative but to do just that. 'Come on, Gerry,' said his ma, 'give us G. H. Chirgwin.' With a bulging neck and his eyes closed, Gerry gave a rendering of 'My fiddle is my sweetheart'. He then came forward with 'I am but a poor blind boy'. Tears flowed from Gerry's ma, but all agreed (including Gerry) that 'songs like that wanted a bit of singing'. My older brother finished up by singing a real heartbreaker called 'When I lost you'.

The party was now getting tired and it was also late. Everyone had to see about getting a move on because of work tomorrow. All except Gerry. 'No bleeding work was going to see him tomorrow.' Gerry's ma and stepfather thanked Mum for such a wonderful time and hoped Gerry and Mary would make a go of things. They had to get the last bus to Homerton. 'Battered Face' carried the gramophone and Gerry's ma the horn. Goodness knows how they managed to squeeze on a bus! We all went to bed tired. It had been a hectic day. Early Monday morning my father staggered out at five o'clock. He started the day with his 'rum and milk', and then to work. Jo' gave us all a cup of tea about seven o'clock, taking care not to wake the bride and groom. Poor Mum was left to clear up the mess left over, with the despondent prospect of trying to make ends meet in the forthcoming week. This turned out to be a disaster for all. My watch went back to hock and

Sid behind the counter generously lent Mum three shillings on it. I never saw it again. Next day, Gerry got pinched for stealing a bike. It just goes to show.

Chapter Two

THINGS looked very bad for Gerry when he appeared in Court on a charge of stealing a bicycle. He had no previous convictions, but there had been such a spate of stolen bicycles that the magistrate was making an example of anyone who was caught. He was remanded and due to appear at Old Street Police Court the following Monday. My father kept on to Mum about Gerry being a thief. He forecast a criminal future for him. Yet, who was a bigger rogue than he, himself? Mum reminded him of this and said the day would come when he would be caught, which he was.

Poor Mary was distraught. No money was coming in, and it was all left to my mother to help her, keep us all, pay the rent and do everything in general. To get a few shillings she would make up a few children's bonnets, and my sister Jo' and I would go to any neighbour who had children and try to sell them. Very often I would come home from school and there was nothing to eat until one of us effected a sale.

Once, I remember, Mum told me I would have to have the morning off from school and go to Wilmer Gardens and ask Mrs. Johnson, an old friend of hers, if she would like to buy a bonnet for her eldest girl. I got there about nine-thirty in the morning, walked in and went upstairs. Being tenements, anyone could walk in. I knocked on the door and Mrs. Johnson told me to come in. I shall never forget the sight that met my eyes. There was no furniture of any sort in the room, just a tea-chest and an orange box. A few wooden embers were on their last in the grate. She looked like a skeleton and was trying to feed her baby on the breast. On the tea-chest was a cup of watery tea and she was crying. The sight of Mrs. Johnson has never been out of my memory. Between tears, she asked me what I wanted. I told her Mum had sent me to see if she would like to buy a bonnet for one and threepence. The poor woman was starving. It seemed Mr. Johnson was 'inside' and the broker's men had been in and stripped the place of everything in order to get the rent that was owing. There wasn't a thing left. This was at a time when England had the greatest empire the world had ever known, yet most of the working population were living below workhouse level.

Gerry duly appeared at Old Street and Mary had been advised to attend. After hearing the case, the magistrate told him that his criminal activities must be curbed and that a stiff prison sentence was the only way of teaching him a lesson. My sister told the magistrate he was a good husband and pleaded that, being his first offence, he should treat him with leniency. The beak saw my sister was due to have a baby and told Gerry that it was due to his wife that the original sentence he was going to impose (six months) would be cut to three months. Poor Mary was heartbroken. Mum and Jo' were crying when they got home. Mum told Mary she would try and see her through until Gerry was released and the time would soon pass. What a tower of strength my mother was! There was no help from my father; he carried on in his own drunken way and had no feeling for any of us. To us, the children, he somehow didn't exist. We seldom saw him. It was only at week-ends that his presence was felt. He would start on us over something trivial and we would go and stand round Mum. We knew we were safe when she was around.

The following weeks were very bad for us all. We were behind with the rent and saw no way of paying up. One Friday dinner-time, a loud knock on the door sent me running to open it. A huge man was standing there. 'Is your mother in?' he asked. Before I could call Mum he was in. He announced he was taking over until the rent was paid. He was the dreaded 'Broker's Man'. Poor Mum. She burst into tears. She just did not know where to turn. The man took up his position in an armchair and again emphasised the point that he would remain until the rent was forthcoming. This was the second time in my young life that I had seen the Broker's Man. The first time they took everything we had except bedding. Mum did not want this to happen again. We could only wait until the old man came home. Being Friday night, this was about seven o'clock. Mum explained what had happened but all he said was, 'I've got no bloody money, let them take the home if they want to,' and walked out. What a man.

Mum sent Jo' to my grandmother to try and borrow some money. Grandma used to teach the violin and piano and wasn't too badly off. She came back with Jo' and paid the Broker's Man off. Mum's people were fairly well off, but wouldn't have much to do with us owing to my father. If she would leave him, they were prepared to help in any way, but not while she stayed with him.

We now had to consider moving again. Mum saw a large flat in Rotherfield Street, Essex Road, but the snag was there was not enough room for us all. The rent was only six shillings a week and Mum couldn't miss it, so she suggested Mary should try to get a couple of rooms somewhere. She could then make a fresh start with Gerry when he was released. Mary thought this was a good idea because she did not want Gerry to meet my father when he came home. She found two rooms in a small turning off the Southgate Road. So once again we got the barrow and like nomads we were on the move again.

Our new abode was Ebenezer Buildings, Rotherfield Street. What a dump it was after the nice little house we had just left! It was a basement flat with one large room at the front and two bedrooms at the back. We soon settled in; it was a case of having to. Mary moved at the same time, but she didn't fancy sleeping on her own at first. Some nights she would pack in with us. After a while, she had to get used to the idea of going home to sleep, we hardly had enough room for ourselves. When she started to go to her own place she insisted on me going with her. I used to like that. It was nice and quiet and she used to make a fuss of me. In the mornings she would wake me with a cup of tea and give me a breakfast with whatever she could muster, then off I'd go to school and Mary would go to Mum.

Jo' was working in a factory off the Southgate Road

making Christmas crackers and she earned about ten shillings a week. She would say to me on Friday mornings, 'Meet me tonight and I'll take you to Manze's.' On Friday night I would be outside the factory gate. Out would come Jo', take my hand and off we would go to Manze's. This was an eel and pie shop in Hoxton Street. Jo' would go up to the counter and ask for a 'pie and half' twice. This was a meat pie and mashed potatoes with gravy. They cost three-ha'pence each. I felt on top of the world and would sit among the grown-ups and enjoy every mouthful. If Jo' could afford it, we would finish up with a fruit pie for a penny. She was a good sort. After the 'nosh up' we would go home. Jo' would give Mum her money and start on the housework.

The old man was still coming home drunk. Weekends were the worst. One Sunday night, we were all home and the old man came in paralytic drunk. He tried to get his boots off and somehow a bag of silver fell out of his pocket. 'That's not my bloody money,' he said, 'it's Peggy's.' Peggy was his foreman. We all knew different. To make it look right, he asked Jo' to count it to make sure it was all correct. He said Jo' was the 'only one he could trust'. Jo' proceeded to count. Every now and then she would slip two shillings or half-a-crown in her apron. After the count he told her to tie it up as he 'had to pay it in the morning'. When he went to bed Jo' passed over to Mum anything she'd managed to knock off. This sort of thing happened on several occasions. We always had a good feed the next day.

These were the days of half sovereigns. One day

Mum told me to get a threepenny bottle of gold paint. I asked her what she wanted it for and she told me 'never you mind and hurry up'. That night my father came home drunk as usual. He never hung about. He always went off to bed. Drunk as he was, he always had enough sense to slip his money bag under his side of the mattress. When all was quiet Mum slipped in to see if he had 'gone off'. When she was sure he was asleep she slipped her hand gently under the mattress and withdrew the bag. She then had to work fast in case he woke up. Out came half a sovereign, in went a painted sixpence. She would then creep in the bedroom and slip the bag back. The amazing thing about all this was we never heard another word about it.

Time was getting close for Gerry's release from prison. It was also near time for Mary's baby to be born. If the baby came before Gerry's release she was going to have it at our place. If Gerry came out first she would have it at home and Mum would look after her. The old man forbade Mary to bring Gerry to our home. He wasn't going to have any bleeding thieves in his house. Gerry was released before the baby was born. The morning he came out the poor chap just did not know what to do. He didn't want to face the old man, knowing there would be trouble, so he walked the streets for some time, waiting for him to go to work. About half past seven we heard stones being thrown up at the window. When Mum got up she saw Gerry standing outside. She immediately let him in, made him some tea and gave him something to eat. From his pocket he took out a small brown loaf, which was like a brick. It seems in those days the prisoners were given them on release. It was a tearful reunion. He promised Mum he would never do anything wrong again and, given a chance, he would make good. Some time during that day Mary and Gerry went back to their own place as they didn't want any trouble with the old man. When he came home, Mum told him that Gerry was home, and threatened to 'brain him' if he started any trouble. He did eventually see Gerry, but both trod very warily. Gerry tried several ways to get a living and things were tough for him. He chopped and sold firewood, and tried 'Ragging' but wasn't very successful. Eventually, his stepfather got him a job as a fish fryer with him in a shop at London Fields. Mary's baby was born and was named after my sister Jo'. She was a sweet little thing and we all loved her very much.

Meanwhile, things were catching up with my father. He was beginning to suffer from gout and was having days off from work. This didn't help him at all and his mates were losing out. If he didn't go to work they could not operate the swindles they were working on deliveries.

The shop Gerry worked at was a large wet and dry fish shop owned and run by a Jewish family. Gerry worked well under his step-father's supervision. He also got friendly with the owner's son, who had been a bit of a villain in his time but was now kept on a tight rein by his parents. One day while they were cleaning and cutting fish, Harry the son was telling Gerry how he would like to get his hands on some of the takings that were going into the till. The trouble was, he said, that he needed help and there had been no one he could trust. If he could find someone he could make it worth everyone's while. Gerry asked him what scheme he had in mind and he explained.

When the shop was busy, the accomplice was to come in the shop as an ordinary customer and ask for ha'penny worth of chips. But he must wait to be served by Harry, who would then serve the chips, at the same time dropping two shillings or a half-crown into the paper. The accomplice would then depart, walk down the alley at the side, sort out the money from the chips and be prepared to come in again. This would go on all night until a signal from Harry told him to go home. The money would then be collected by Gerry and shared out. The question was, who could they trust to carry out the scheme?

Gerry told Mary of Harry's scheme and she also thought it a good one. Mary approached Mum and told her all about it and wondered if she would allow me to be the accomplice. Mum told her in no mean way that she would not allow her boy to be mixed up in Gerry's bloody swindles. The schemers were now despondent, and another approach was made to Mum. Fish and chips were suggested instead of chips alone.

In the end Mum let me go, but 'Gawd help the sods if the boy gets in any trouble'. I expect Mum was thinking of the fish and chip meals I would be bringing home. I was about nine years old at the time and knew enough about life to know what I was doing. On the appointed day to start, I went home with Mary and got introduced to Harry. He looked a real villain. He convinced me I had nothing to worry about and I would get a treat at the end of each week. Next night I started. I was given some coppers to buy the fish and chips. When the shop got busy, in I went. I could hardly reach the counter and Harry had a job to see me among the customers. When he spotted me he'd say, 'Yes, sonny?' I'd say, 'Ha'penny and ha'porth,' get my fish and chips, walk out, sort out the money from the fish and chips and then proceed to eat them if I was hungry, which I nearly always was. I would do this several times each night, taking great care not to let Harry's mother see me too often. I also carried a bag in my pocket for the fish and chips that I couldn't eat. When I was given the signal 'go home' I would call in at Mary's and give her the money. She would then see me home. When I arrived they would all raid me. Saturday came and I was given sixpence or a shilling. This didn't work much of a financial proposition for me, but I stuck it out as the fish and chips helped out at home. After a few weeks Gerry told me I wasn't to go any more. It seemed that a drastic drop in the takings had taken place and Harry was suspected. So ended a big deal.

Mary and Gerry continued to see us, taking care not to see too much of the old man. Little Jo' was getting on fine. She was developing into a lovely baby and we all loved her very much; even the old man was beginning to take notice of her. By this time, my eldest brother Will was on his way to Australia where he was to stay for two years. Before leaving he had asked Mum if his young lady could stay with us for a few days. We scarcely had room for ourselves, let alone another grown-up, but Mum hadn't liked to refuse so she wrote to the girl explaining the position. Unfortunately, however, the young lady wrote back saying that she so wanted to see us all that she just did not mind about sleeping, as anywhere would suit her. Before we knew what day it was her trunk had arrived and Nancy followed. She intended, by the look of things, to make it a permanent stay. She had been in service at Surbiton and had packed up and was going to take potluck with us. Goodness knows what my brother had told her. She must have thought we were better off than we were. She shared Jo's bed and seemed a jolly sort of girl. She helped out with the chores, but had no income of any kind. She stayed for a few weeks and then started to date different men. Mum didn't like this and had to tell her to go. As far as I can remember nothing more was ever heard of her. So much for Nancy.

My brother Bert was getting himself in trouble with the police. He got caught with two other lads busting into someone's house. His intelligence was pretty low and he was easily led. He came home from the 'burglary' with two tame mice and a pair of eyeglasses! This was too much for Mum and she explained to the Court that she was making application to get him away on a training ship. He got off on condition he went away. The old man and Mum had to take him to the City, I think it was Clarke Place, Bishopsgate. He was accepted for training on the *Warspite* at Greenhithe, Kent. After a few days they sent for him. We were all in tears when he went, but Mum held back hers. She had to make us see it was for his own good that he went. We heard from him after a few days and all felt better. He made the best of it and after a while he learned to become a drummer. I always remember him coming to London to play in the *War-*

spite band for the Lord Mayor's Show. He was also a brilliant swimmer and won several prizes and medals. Mum was certainly right to send him away. God knows how he would have finished up if she hadn't.

On more than one occasion I had to stay away from school because I had no boots. The terrible part of all this was my father who was still coming home the worse for drink and had money in his pocket (though how much of it had been honestly come by I do not know). One day I took a note to school asking the teacher to excuse my absence the previous day, due to the rain and the fact that I had no serviceable boots. The teacher must have had a word with one of the better-off boys and next morning I was called out of class. He took me to the lobby and asked me to try on an old pair of boots. I knew the boy who had given them and wished the ground would open and swallow me up. Every time I saw that boy I had the feeling he was telling his mates I was wearing his boots.

My sister Jo' made life as happy as she could for my young sister Molly and myself. Sometimes on a Monday night she would come home from work and if she had a few coppers left over from the week-end she would say to Mum, 'Get yourself and the kids ready, we're going up the Brit.' This was the old Britannia Theatre in Hoxton. Jo' loved the dramas that were performed there. If Mum could afford it we had a bag of peanuts or a ha'penny bag of sweets. We went in the 'gallery' for twopence—half-price for us kids. Among the dramas I remember was *The Face at the Window* —real horrible. Others were *Sweeney Todd, Maria Marten, Why Girls Leave Home*. Many times I have lain awake after going to the Brit, terrified to open my eyes for fear of seeing the murdered lying next to me. Sometimes we went to Collins Music Hall or the Islington Empire. That was different. They always had variety shows. We saw Harry Champion, Vesta Tilley, The Two Bobs, Hetty King, comedians of all sorts and stars of the day. We always dreaded coming home after these outings. The old man would start a row as soon as we entered the door. He thought Mum should always be at his beck and call. Jo' got to the age when she would stand no nonsense from him. As soon as he started to create she would stand up to him and defy him to touch any one of us. He was a crafty old devil and he knew how far to go. Mum had a good ally in Jo'. About February 1914 he had an accident at work. He cut the top of his finger off and had to stay at home. No money was forthcoming. Not that he ever gave us much; six or seven shillings was the most he ever gave Mum. Now she also had to keep him, so to help out she got herself a job making ladies' coats. Before she went out in the morning she left him some money to get dinners for us children. All we ever had from him was bread and marge or bread and jam. The rest of the money he'd spend at the local pub.

One night she asked us what we had had for dinner and one of us told her. She nearly went mad. When he came home that night he got the biggest hiding a woman could possibly give a man. But he was no man. She called him all the 'starving gits' she could lay her tongue to. (That was a favourite word of Mum's when she was angry.) She wouldn't go back to work after that. She explained to the firm what had happened and they gave her some work to do at home. She would save all the cloth cuttings and when things got really bad and she had no money I would be detailed to take them to a rag shop in St. John's Road and see how much I could get for them. She sorted the woollens from the cottons and I got more for them that way than I would have got if they had been mixed. If the old boy was in a good mood I would get sixpence or eightpence. I was then instructed to 'go down Hoxton' and get 6 lb of potatoes, 1 lb onions and 1½ lb of 'back fat'. This would come to about fivepence. Mum would then cut the fat into small pieces and fry it, mash up the potatoes, pour the fat in the middle and mix the lot up. Small pieces of onion would then be fried brown and these she would mix in also. We would then have a plateful each and we really felt we had had something to eat. We often used to say to Mum, 'When are we going to have a mixed dinner, Mum?' Her reply would be. 'See how much money we have when you come out from school.' If there was no money it would be bread and jam. The old man eventually went back to work and spent what compensation money he got on drink.

About this time we had a visit from Gerry who came in one night frantic with worry. He told Mum little Jo' had got pneumonia and was in a bad way. Could she go back with him at once. Mum wouldn't leave my sister Molly and I so we all went home with Gerry. The old man cut up rough about us all going. Mum called him a wicked and selfish old sod to talk like that on such a sad occasion. When we got to Mary's, Gerry had to go back to work. The fish shop was open to midnight and he had to be there to clean up. Poor little Jo' was in a bad way and the doctor didn't hold out much hope. Mary, Mum and Jo' were crying, and Mary begged us not to leave her. Arrangements were made to stop the night. My sister and I were put to bed while all the others slept in chairs. But there was no sleep for anyone. Little Jo' died during the night. Their eyes were red with crying and loss of sleep. Mum pulled everyone together and we all went back to our place. Gerry was left to make arrangements with the local undertaker. I am sure little Jo' was not insured. Gerry had to appeal to the boss's son Harry to help him out, which he did. After the funeral Mary and Gerry moved to a flat in Hackney Road. The place they had gave too many memories of the baby.

Towards the summer of 1914 Nemesis was catching up with the old man. He had the gout really badly and could not go to work. He had to stay in bed for six weeks. He had never been so ill. Mum had to struggle again. It was purgatory for the old man to stay in bed. He couldn't drink and he was afraid of losing his job. He had need to be worried. They gave someone else the job of delivering goods and it didn't take the chap long to see what was going on. He blew the gaff to the boss and all who had been concerned got the sack. He was well and truly worried when his partners in crime called in and told him what had happened. The firm hadn't made up their minds about prosecution. He told Mum that when he was able to get up he might have to go to prison. Her words to him were, 'Serve you bloody well right. The biggest rogue gets caught in the end.' He got no sympathy from Mum. His panel money had been delayed and when it did come through Mum asked the insurance man if he could let her have it. He said he couldn't do that, as the old man had to sign for it. It was about £4. He went in the bedroom to see him, paid him and went. Mum goes in after and asks the old man, 'What about it?' 'What about what?' he says. 'The bloody insurance money,' says Mum. 'He only gave me fifteen shillings,' says the old man, 'the other's not come through yet.' She called him all the old tykes and rotters she could think of, but it was no use, he would not part up. She managed to get four shillings or five shillings out of him and had to let it go at that.

He was now staked and wanted a drink. He called me in his bedroom and told me to get him a 'quart of ale and hurry up'. I was not old enough to go inside the pub, so the procedure was to wait outside and when someone went in to ask them if they would please get the beer. I had done this on several occasions. This particular night I got the beer in a quart can with a wire handle. Going home I would swing the can, that was now full up, a full circle the length of my arm. This I had done several times and was now an expert, or thought I was. I was merrily swinging the beer when suddenly the handle parted company from the can and the beer went in the road. I was petrified with fear at what the old man would do to me when I got home. When I arrived I told Mum what had happened. 'A bloody good job,' she said. 'But how am I going to tell him?' I asked. 'Come with me,' she said, and in we went. When she told him what had happened his face went purple. He called me all the 'daft bleeders' he could think of. 'Serves you bloody well right, you shouldn't send a child for beer,' said Mum. I thanked God that he couldn't get up. Anyhow, he got his beer in the end. Jo' went to save the peace.

One night during that week, when we had all gone to bed, there was a terrific scuffle in the road. The old man just could not keep his nose out of a fight, it somehow fascinated him. He woke Mum up and said, 'Ann, there ain't half a bloody fight going on outside.' Half asleep she replied, 'Mind your own business and go to sleep, it's nothing to do with you.' Although he could hardly move, he somehow managed to get himself to the street door and stood there in his pants and socks for quite a while. While he is watching the fight, Mum goes to turn over and to get to sleep, when she feels her leg touch something. She grabs it and when she looks it's the old man's panel money. He had hidden it in his sock and it fell out when he got up. Mum immediately tumbled what it was and hid it in her nightdress. After the fight the old man gets back to bed and off to sleep.

Next morning Mum gets up and gives him a cup of tea. As she gets near the door she sees him through the crack looking all over the bed. 'Have you lost something?' says Mum. 'Don't look so bloody innocent,' says the old man, 'you know what I've lost.' 'How should I know?' says Mum. 'I had a few bob left out of my panel money and if it's not here you've bleeding well pinched it,' was the old man's comment. 'Where did you keep it?' says Mum. 'In me bloody sock,' said the old man and he was now blue in the face. 'Well,' said Mum, 'you shouldn't have poked your nose into that fight last night. If it's lost, you lost it then.' He had us look all over the place for it. What a time Mum gave us next day! I had new boots, Molly new shoes and Jo' wasn't forgotten either. The old man never would say how much he lost.

As he got better he would somehow manage to get to the local pub. He still had his panel money coming in. In the end that got stopped. A Health Visitor called one night and he was out. That was his lot. The Visitor's report went in and they stopped his money. He now had to think about a job. He still reckoned his firm owed him a week's wages. He wrote out a note asking his foreman to pay his son any money due to him and told me to come with him to deliver the note. I remember the road but not the name of the firm. We walked to Danbury Street, Islington. We got to the place and he told me to go through a wicket gate, ask for the foreman and deliver the note. I had instructions that should the foreman ask where he was, I was to say he was ill in bed. He retired out of sight with hopes running high. I went in the gate, asked for the foreman and gave him the note. I waited quite a while for a reply. The foreman eventually came out and gave me twopence and told me to mind the road going home and give this note to Dad. I found the old man and gave him the note. He read it and was livid. He never said a word to me. When I got home, Mum asked me 'if I got the old man's money'. I told her about the letter. He still hadn't told Mum the contents. She found the letter eventually in his pocket. It was worded to the effect that they had thought the matter over and if it wasn't for his having a wife and children he would have had to answer to the law for his thieving in the past, and they warned him never to show himself near the firm again.

He now had to get himself a job. The First World War had broken out and things were looking grim. All Mum's friends were calling in, crying that their husbands had been called up from the reserves. They all came to us with their troubles.

The only job the old man could find was in a timber mill at King's Cross. Now he really knew what work was all about! He used to come home with his shoulders raw from humping timber. This didn't stop him from boozing. He kept all his money, but he had to go easy during the week as he only had what he earned and no longer had any chance of fiddling. When he was young he had belonged to the Volunteers—some form of Territorial Army—with a good excuse to go drinking. He had a framed certificate on the wall to the effect that he had passed his drill instruction. He was always boasting to people that if it wasn't for us he would 'join up tomorrow'. The times I've heard him arguing with people as to how the war should be fought and won. His point of argument was 'there was no force in the world that could beat a British square'. He just wasn't capable of thinking beyond the Zulu War. One Saturday night, half cut as usual, he was boasting how he would 'join up tomorrow if it wasn't for his commitments'. Mum overheard him and asked him what he considered commitments. 'Surely you can leave the pub, which is the only commitment I know you have.' She also called him a coward and told him in no uncertain words that 'he didn't have the guts of a louse'. 'Am I?' he said. 'Jan,' meaning me, 'write this letter as I tell you.' Being anxious for him to go, I got paper and pen and wrote as he dictated. I even took his certificate from the Volunteers and enclosed that with the letter and sent it to Whitehall. He knew they wouldn't have him. Back came a letter saying he was too old. We were all disappointed.

One morning Mary and Gerry's mother called. They were both crying. Unbeknown to them he had packed up his job at the fish shop and joined up. He was called up that morning.

Chapter Three

GERRY joining up was a shock to us in every way. He had always been against the army. No bloody army would get him, he would say. I think his job in the fish shop was the reason. He worked very long hours: nine o'clock in the morning, home again at three o'clock, on again at five o'clock and there he was until midnight. Joining the army was an escape for him. This had now put Mum in a spot. Mary would not stay on her own after losing little Jo'. She just could not settle down. We hardly had enough room for ourselves. So Mum suggested we try for another place to live and all be together. Flats were not large enough for us all. One afternoon, Mum and Mary went househunting. After looking at several, they decided on a house in Loanda Street—No. 15. This was a small house by the side of the Regents Canal near the bridge in Kingsland Road. By taking this house we had a room for Mary. They thought the war wouldn't last long and when it was over and Gerry came out of the army they could get another place of their own.

We couldn't move on a barrow this time. With Gerry and Bert away, this only left me, and I was too small to attempt it. We had to have a horse and van. In those days a notice-board was in every greengrocer's shop stating 'Horse & Van 1/3d. per hour'. Mum reckoned if we packed everything ourselves it would only take three to four hours. We order the horse and van: it was something new for us. We must have thought we were the aristocracy after previous moves with a barrow.

We settled in at the new address and the first night we were kept awake with bugs. They came from every crack in the wallpaper. When the landlord had the place decorated they must have papered over the bugs. Mum had a friend living two doors away, who suggested we got some carbolic. I went and got a 'pennorth of carbolic' and Mum and her friend went bug-hunting. They also sealed up one room at a time and got some sulphur candles going. This kept them down, but it was a job to get rid of them altogether. In those days nearly everyone had bugs and it was usually a question of keeping them down rather than expecting to be completely free of them.

I had to change schools and went to Haggerston Road School. Of all the schools I had been to, this was the toughest. Both as regards the teachers and the boys who attended. One was for ever trying to keep out of trouble. I could usually hold my own with most of the boys whatever school I went to, but these were the toughest villains I ever knew. I got the measure of most of them in the end and after a fight or two, and a caning from the headmaster, I was accepted as one of them. I was also invited to go 'scrumping' for fruit down Spitalfields Market, but had to decline the offer as this could only be done during the dinner hour when I was nearly always wanted at home. In any case my mother forbade me to get mixed up with a bad crowd.

I could see the wisdom of her words. On more than one occasion a boy would be missing from school for a week or two. When he came back he'd had his hair cropped short, like an old-time convict, and we knew he had been in a Remand Home.

The old man changed his job after the move. He 'wasn't going all the soddin' way to King's Cross'. So he got himself a job at a local timber yard by the name of King & Scarborough in the Kingsland Road, again humping timber. I used to sit on the wall for hours watching the men stack the timber. One day a film company set up their gear and were filming a thriller. The actors were jumping from stack to stack, and when the hero caught the villain a fight ensued and the villain got slung in the water. It was thrilling to watch. The old man wasn't earning so much money and couldn't get as drunk as he used to. One day he suggested to Mum he would like to come home to dinner as he was so near home. He would pay Mum any extra money it cost. After the first week, however, he never kept his promise and Mum wouldn't stand for it any more. He just did not like paying out.

In order to keep things going, Mum said she would like to start a small shop. She could then make up boys' trousers, girls' frocks and pinafores, etc. After giving the matter much thought, I was told to go and get two orange boxes and two apple boxes. I took a mate with me and went down Hoxton to get the boxes. Mum said she was going to turn the front room into a shop. In those days no planning permission was needed. Between Mum and myself we made a platform and sidewings, got some wallpaper, and in no time had our shop-front. Mum made dresses, trousers and all kinds of children's wear.

When they were set out it looked very nice. Neighbours used to pay off a sixpence or a shilling, and when they paid up got the goods. This was all right but she had started to run out of materials to make clothes up with. Her sister had married a chap who owned a clothing factory in Camden Passage, Islington. He used to employ girls making dresses and coats. He was in a fair way of business. Mum went to see them and arranged to buy up all the off-cuts of material. These were triangle-shaped pieces and were in bundles. He wouldn't give them to her, but offered to sell them at so much a bundle. He was dead mean. Here was her own brother-in-law who had all the money he needed, his own two houses and servants, yet was too mean to let my mother have these without paying for them. How low my uncle was in my eyes, he'll never know! The problem was how to get the stuff home; they were heavy. She mentioned this to the old man and it was suggested that I go once a week to collect them. I didn't know my way to Camden Passage, so the old man showed me the way. He took me all round the back doubles and I found it was no mean walk. I had to have something to put the bundles in. Mum gave me a few coppers and I went to the local rag shop for a pair of old pram wheels and axle, got a sugar box from the grocer at the corner and made myself a cart. Once every week after school, Mum would get me something to eat and off I would go to Camden Passage. My uncle would take the money and give me the bundle and then I'd start to walk home. It took me the best part of three hours to get there and back. Many's the time I got soaked to the skin. But Mum did appreciate the help I was giving her.

Going to Camden Passage I would have to pass Edie's Bar. Here one could get a large cup of tea and a lump of 'Tottenham' cake for a penny. If I could get a penny before leaving I would pull up at Edie's and have a tea and cake and really enjoy it. It was a very popular place and was always crowded with poor people. The carmen used to put up there and it was so crowded that one could very seldom get a seat.

Mum's shop was taking just about enough to exist on. Sometimes she would be on the machine until midnight. It wasn't much of a life for us. Mary got herself a job at De-Leefs in Kingsland Road and when she and Jo' came home at night they had to get everything ready themselves. The old man could see Mum had a few bob coming in and he stopped giving her the six or seven shillings that he had done in the past. There were rows every week-end. He still came home drunk on Saturday and Sunday, and life was really unbearable.

Gerry was stationed at Woolwich and came home week-ends if he could, but he was getting fed up. He missed his freedom. One week-end when he was planning to come home his leave got stopped. They had put him on a recruiting drive. The district he was coming to was Hoxton. He wrote a card to Mary explaining why he couldn't get home. I had heard about this drive and thought I would go and see it. He was in the R.H.A. and mounted on horseback. I was standing in Hoxton High Street when the parade came along. There was a mounted band followed by the soldiers on horseback, followed by the marching infantry. I saw Gerry on his horse and waved to him. He couldn't stop but beckoned to me. I ran alongside of him and he told me they would be stopping at Pitfield Street later that night and to tell Mary to meet him there at a certain time. It was very important. I got the message back to Mary and she went along to find him. She came back very worried. She told Mum he was fed up with the army and he was going to desert. The old man created when he heard about it. He threatened to give him away to the police. 'He wasn't going to have any bleeding deserters in his house.' Gerry did desert and he was on the run. The police came several times. Looking back, one can't help feeling sorry for him. One night there was a knock on the door and when I opened it there was Gerry. He ran in quick, shut the door and said, 'Is the old 'un in?' He frightened the life out of me. He was dishevelled and dirty. 'No, the old man's out,' I said. With that, he ran upstairs to Mary and it was tragic to see them in each other's arms. The police must have been watching. They knocked a few minutes after Gerry. Gerry guessed who it was, jumped out of the back window and was away. They never caught him.

To crown all, my brother Bert came home from the *Warspite* training ship. He had finished his training and was going in the Merchant Navy. Ships were being sunk in great numbers by the Germans and none of us felt too good about it. Mum said, 'If anything happens to him, I'll never forgive myself.' She couldn't get it out of her mind that by putting him away on the *Warspite* she was somehow responsible. He didn't seem to mind and to ease her mind said he would have gone in the Merchant Navy anyway. The police were still looking for Gerry and the word had got around to the neighbours. The boys at school had got to know and I had many a bust-up defending him.

Everything was now getting too much for Mum and she reckoned the house had a curse on it. The only way out was to move again. This time she found a house in Scawfell Street. This wasn't far from Loanda Street. It certainly looked a road with some life in it, which was what we were used to. Loanda Street was a drab place of flat-fronted houses where everyone closed their doors. There wasn't the friendliness. So we moved again, with horse and van. The new house had three rooms down and four up. It was the first house in the road and next door was a huge stable belonging to Thos. Cook & Son. Many horses and brakes were stabled there, which proved of great interest to me. There was also a small garden. Mary had the front room upstairs and lived with us. It looked as if it was going to be a happy house.

We hadn't been in long before Gerry arrived, just as if nothing had happened. The police were off his tail and he somehow seemed to have got away with it. He got himself a job and was now leading a normal life. The old man also got himself another job. He went to see some of his old cronies around Shoreditch and he got in as a timber salesman. He had a pony and trap and was doing well. He seemed in the money again. Not that it made much difference to us as he still kept it to himself.

We were now well into 1915 and several commodities were in short supply. Among them were screws and glue. If any could be obtained a good price could be had from the small cabinet-makers in the district. Gerry and the old man were on friendly terms and were now going out to the local to have a drink together. Evidently, during their drinking bouts, the old man told Gerry what a wonderful market there was for

screws and glue and how he wished he could get hold of some. Gerry was working in the Bethnal Green Road, making munition boxes. Plenty of screws and glue were used in their construction. Gerry reckoned he could get plenty but some arrangement would have to be made to collect them. He could get them out during his afternoon tea break, but not dinner-time or night-time. I was approached and asked to go each day to meet Gerry during his afternoon tea break. Mum went mad when she knew what they were up to, but between the two of them they managed to convince her there was no risk. I had to take a shopping bag to school with me and then proceed to Bethnal Green Road at four o'clock. I can't remember the name of the pub where I had to meet Gerry. At the side of the pub there was a gent's toilet that was always open. When Gerry came along I would dive in and he would follow. He would quickly undo his apron and take out packets of screws and packets of dried glue from inside his trousers. He also had his pockets stuffed. They were quickly dropped in the bag and I would walk home. This I had to do every day of the week and Saturday mornings also. The old man would take them on his round and flog them to various small cabinet-makers. On Saturday afternoons they would share out the proceeds. I don't remember ever getting anything out of this, but I suppose I must have done. Mum wouldn't have let me do it for nothing. It's a marvel I didn't grow up a criminal the things I had to do for them.

On Saturday, Gerry and the old man, who were now the best of friends, would go drinking in a pub at the corner of Weymouth Terrace. We now had a front room again and many's the drunken parties we had. Mum would sometimes go with Mary for a drink on Saturday nights and the old man would treat them to anything they would care to drink, but he still wouldn't give her a penny for the home. Mum didn't drink much. She would have a gin and clove, and then try to get a seat near the corner. The old man would call up for drinks and often forget his change. The barman knew Mum and when this happened he would give Mum a wink and a nod and push it over towards her. She had her reasons for going.

Mum decided to start selling clothes again. One Friday she said to me, 'Jan, I want you to go down Hoxton in the morning and see if you can find a site where we can pitch a stall.' The market was usually chock-a-block with stalls but this didn't deter her from sending me to have a look round. I started from the 'narrow way' of Hoxton and walked along towards Old Street, but couldn't see many vacant places. Coming back, I saw somewhere that took my eye. In the centre of the road between Nuttall Street and Wilmer Gardens were two public lavatories, flanked all round by a wide pavement. There were two or three stalls there but plenty of room for more. Home I went and told Mum. This pleased her and she thought she could do all right there. So I had to start the walk to Camden Passage again. But I had lost my cart. Some time ago I had to go to Whiston Street Gasworks for three pen'orth of coke. To get the coke I went in the gate, paid my threepence in the office and got a ticket. I then went to where the men were filling the sacks, got loaded and went back to where I had left my cart. When I got there someone had pinched it. I should have known better. The lads round there could take your laces out of your boots and you wouldn't know they were gone. I had to carry the coke home and swore I would somehow get my cart back. Mary was expecting another baby and had bought a second-hand pram. I had to borrow the pram and push it to Camden Passage, get loaded and push it all the way home. I felt a 'Charley' pushing that pram, but the thought of tea and cake at Edie's Bar was the carrot that kept the donkey going. Mum worked hard all that week and bought and mended any old clothes she could find and got them ready for the stall on the coming Saturday.

Opposite the house where we lived was a coal shop and they had a couple of barrows which they let out on hire. I booked one for Saturday, when at eight sharp I got it loaded up with two sacks of clothes, old boots and anything Mum thought she could sell. I pushed the barrow and Mum walked alongside of me. I was just hoping the pitch was vacant. It was and I was overjoyed.

I propped up the barrow with the front legs I had brought along with me so that Mum could sit on it. We had some boards and these we laid out on the barrow. Mum unpacked the clothes and we were away. By nine-thirty people were beginning to flock into the market and we soon had some customers. The frocks and pinafores went like wildfire. 'Fifteen pence the frocks,' Mum would say, and 'ninepence the pinafores.' About midday we were half sold out. I asked Mum if she would like some tea. ' 'Ere y'are, son,' she said, and took the money out of the takings. I got a jug of tea and some sandwiches and we ate them ravenously. We'd had no breakfast owing to our having had to start out early. Three o'clock came and we had sold out. Mum told me to stay with the barrow while she went shopping, and came back loaded. She treated me to the pictures and gave me money to buy sweets. I had never known such times.

Jo' was working in a factory at Shoreditch, also

making munition boxes. The work was hard and it didn't seem to agree with her. Several times she went to the doctor who advised her to change her job, but she still carried on.

Mum was now working harder in order to keep the stall going. I was still going to my uncle's to get the cuttings, and Mum also visited the local 'Tot Shops' to see if she could buy up any second-hand bits that she could earn a few bob on. If old boots had holes in them, we'd mend them. I had some boot-repairing experience. The school used to run a boot-repair class. After school, one could take a penny and the instructor would show us how to repair our boots with pieces of leather. I could only do one in the time allowed, so if both were worn out I would have to go to school the next day with one boot sound and the other with a hole, that could not be mended until the evening. Twenty minutes or so before the class closed there was a panic. Most of us couldn't finish in time and the instructor would work like a trojan finishing our boots since very few of us owned a spare pair. Mum gave me the money to buy a 'hobbin foot' and for one and threepence I got a foot and post and set about mending the boots. They always sold for a few coppers.

We took the stuff out every week and did fairly well. Sometimes, after getting Mum set up, I would go for a walk looking at the shops. Opposite our stall was 'The Land of Promise', as it was called. This was the local workhouse. It was a heart-rending sight to see the old people through the gates. I can never forget it. After a lifetime of hard work these poor old people were left destitute and finished up in this horrible place. Husbands and wives were separated and on Thursdays and Sundays were let out for a few hours. The husband was usually first out and would wait at the gates for his wife. It was heartbreaking to see them embrace each other. The poor old souls were dressed in workhouse fashion. The men had a hard grey suit, cap and heavy boots. The old ladies wore a long skirt and cape with a bonnet that tied under the chin, also all in grey. They would take each other by the arm and walk away, perhaps to relations or the local park.

I have said that next door to our house were the stables of Thos. Cook. In the summer the brakes would leave each morning taking the women from the clubs or pubs on a day's outing. They would start off about eight-thirty in the morning for Chingford, Loughton or Theydon Bois in rural Essex. Each brake was pulled by two or three horses and held about twenty-four people. A man or lad stood on the back to keep the urchins off. One of my school-mates had been out on this trip, as brake-boy, and told me what a good day out it was. The driver had bought his food and given him half the collection, given by the trippers, who were nearly always half-cut coming home. I thought I would like to do this, so I asked Mum if I could have a day off from school and go. She had a word with the driver, who told her I would be all right and I would be looked after, so she agreed.

On the Monday morning I was up bright and early and waited for the brake to come out of the yard. 'Jump on,' said the driver, and away we went. The first of my troubles started as we got round the corner. I saw a load of my class-mates and they were shouting and threatening to tell my teacher where I was. When we picked up the women and they were all in, I squashed my leg in the door, which made tears come to my eyes. All in all I wasn't doing so good. By the time we got to Theydon Bois I wasn't feeling at all happy. The driver didn't give me much to eat and I was really miserable. They started for home about seven o'clock and by the time they had stopped at various pubs, time was getting on. After the last call they passed round the hat, gave the driver the money and I got home about eleven o'clock. The driver gave me sixpence, wished me good night and indoors I went. When I got in, Mum and Jo' were frantic. 'Where have you been all this time?' asked Mum. I told her I could only get home as fast as the horses would bring me and it was no fault of mine if I was late. I also told her I was hungry and she nearly went mad to think I had hardly had anything to eat all day. While she was getting me something ready she asked me how much the driver had given me. When I said sixpence, that done it. 'Come with me, Jo',' she said to my sister, 'no bugger is going to take liberties with my boy.' Down to the stables they went. They asked for the driver, whose name was Tich, went among the horses and found him and gave him hell for leather. He had to give me another half-crown and nearly got done-up in the bargain. It was the last brake ride I ever had.

Chapter Four

GERRY and the old man were still doing well and on Saturday nights they used to celebrate often. Some of their mates were coming home on leave from the trenches, some were covered in mud, and their first stop was the pub nearest to where they lived. Back home they would come with a load of beer and a party was soon in full swing. This usually ended up in a free fight. The old man was always in the thick of it. He'd take up his usual place on the stairs and challenge anyone. He and Gerry were always at it, yet on Sunday morning they'd be the best of pals. 'Coming for a drink, Bill?' Gerry would say. 'Coming now, mate,' the old man would reply, and off they would go as if they had never had a bad word. By dinner-time they had had enough.

Every Sunday dinner-time the old man would come home half-cut and then wait for his dinner. On one occasion he took his coat off and sat by the fire. Mum got the joint out of the oven and started to cut it. Jo' was seeing to the vegetables. He'd been nagging all the time he sat there and as Mum started to cut the meat he must have felt hungry. 'I'll have the first cut,' he said. She gave him one smack with the back of her hand right round his chops. 'Take that. I'll give you first bloody cut,' and with that the force of the clout knocked him in the fireplace. We all started to laugh. It was the most comical sight to see. He went for Jo' because he saw her laughing, and she gave him one. He finished up with nothing and went to bed. This was the sort of thing we had to put up with every Sunday dinner-time. How my mother stuck it out all those years I never know. I have been trying to find the answer to that one for years but haven't found it so far.

Early one morning I was awakened by a baby crying. Mary had given birth to a baby boy. Mum and Jo' had been up all night and were looking very tired. He was a nice little chap and I spent many hours looking after him and taking him out in his pram. After Mary got well she bought herself a sewing-machine and started taking in homework. Twice a week I had to go to Golden Lane and get a bundle of 'Bandoliers'. They were all cut ready for making. It seemed I was now at everyone's beck and call. It was 'Jan go here', 'Jan go there'. I hardly got time to play in the street. Mum reckoned the boys were too rough and I always had to be near in case I was wanted. Some of the lads weren't too bad. Once they knew you could look after yourself if they come any rough stuff, you were accepted. I was invited many times to join them in their street fights, but managed to steer clear. I always had something to do or somewhere to go. These street fights were not funny. A boy would have a fight at school. If he got a pasting, he and his mates would find out where the other boy lived. They would then get together and come *en masse* loaded with bricks, stones or anything they could lay their hands on. Sometimes the other side got wind of what was happening and they would meet them loaded with all sorts of implements. Heads got cut and windows broken. Sometimes the police would be called and a retreat in all directions would take place. Street fights were not for me.

About this time, 1916, Mum was getting worried. She hadn't heard from my brothers and many ships were being sunk. One day Mum and Jo' went to the Admiralty to see why we had heard nothing from my eldest brother. They assured her that all was well.

We were having Zeppelin raids also. Mum wouldn't let us go to bed too early and in the summer we would all sit on the coping at the side of the house where all the neighbours would also congregate; it helped to pass the time. The old man bought himself a bottle of *Liquid Sunshine* rum. He said it would come in handy in case anyone felt queer during an air-raid. One Saturday night he came home half-cut and the warning went. Police would come round with a card on their chest which said 'Take Cover' and blow their whistles. We all went to the door to see what was happening when, suddenly, a gun went off. The old man shot upstairs for his rum. He came tearing down again and wanted to know 'Who had pinched his bleeding rum'. 'You'll leave it alone,' said Mum. She had hidden it. He was blowing his top. He reckoned he was feeling ill and in the end she had to give it to him. Every time a bang went he had a drop more rum. Suddenly in the sky we saw a small red glow which gradually got bigger. It was a Zeppelin coming down in flames. Everyone cheered and the old man celebrated by drinking all his rum. So much for his concern for anyone who might feel queer in a later raid! Next morning we read the Zeppelin had been shot down by Lt. Robinson and had landed at Cuffley, in Hertfordshire.

Some nights the lads would sit on the coping and start singing and wake up Mary's baby. Mum would ask them to clear off. They usually went without comment. One night they were singing alto and treble at the top of their voices and Mum asked them to go. They wouldn't move. She lost all patience in the end and got a big jug of water and slung the lot out of the window. It drenched the lot. The look on their faces was one of amazement and disgust. 'Aw, Mrs. J., you didn't ought to have done that,' they said. 'Serves you bloody well right,' said Mum, 'and if you start again tomorrow night you'll get some more.' I think they had a lot of respect for her after that. She only had to open the window if they started anything and they would shut up like clams. She thought the world of those lads really and often used to ask them in for a cup of tea. They always knew where they stood with her.

About this time, my young sister Molly was starting school. I used to take her to the gate and Mum would meet her at twelve o'clock. I was still at the same school and the masters and teachers were tyrants in my eyes. Looking back, they had something to put up with. They had to be tough to survive. I am sure the discipline they dished out did us the world of good in later years.

We still had our stall in Hoxton, and I used to sit on a box and watch the women shopping. In those days they were treated by their menfolk like serfs. Most of them were dressed in a long skirt and a coarse canvas apron, with an old coat or shawl over their shoulders and a man's cap with a big hatpin on their heads. All their shopping was put in their aprons. Usually there were two or three children tagging along. Somehow they didn't seem to know anything different. Most of them came from poverty-stricken homes and drink was a common cause for misery as well as an escape from it. It needed a strong character like our mum to keep on an even keel.

Mary decided to have the baby christened. She named him after Gerry. On the Sunday she gave a party. It was the usual beer-up. The old man and Gerry dressed up as women and went to the pub like it. They were singing and dancing in the bar and really going to town. They all returned home and went up to Mary's and Gerry's to finish the celebration. They sang and danced and all the ornaments started to fall off the wall. If ever the floor nearly fell in, it did that night. And by way of a change there were no fights. Neighbours couldn't believe it.

The old man was beginning to get the gout again and had to have a few days off. They gave his round to another chap, who called in to see how he was. He just couldn't make out why the pony stopped at every pub. He didn't know my father.

About six o'clock one night I thought I saw a boy with my cart, the one that had been pinched at the Gas Works. I challenged him and he denied it. I went and got Gerry to prove it was mine. Gerry was prepared to give the boy the benefit of the doubt but I knew it was mine. Gerry went indoors again and he was never the same chap in my eyes after that. I was prepared to fight for it, and I did. We were fighting in the middle of the road and I was getting the best of it when a taxi nearly run us over and stopped outside our house. Who should get out but my brother Bert and a mate. I ran up to him and he put his arms round me like elder brothers do. I was too dazed to do anything about my cart. I just remember the boy getting up and running off with it.

My brother's homecoming boosted our morale. It was such a long time since we had seen him. I remember running upstairs and shouting, 'Mum, Bert's home.' She was on the machine at the time and thought I was kidding until he came in. She kissed and cuddled him and could hardly believe it. His mate was much older than my brother. I'd say he was about thirty-five and he was a French Canadian. Tall and broad with a Clark Gable moustache. He could hardly speak English but he made himself understood.

We had a real reunion. My brother looked a lot older and was well tanned. He had been on tankers out East. Mum and Jo' rushed around and got them a meal and after they went to the local for a drink. Everyone went: Gerry, Mary, Jo' and Mum. Needless to say they met the old man. It was a grand slam and everyone came back home. Bert's mate was named Max. He saw the old man liked rum and bought him a bottle. I was sent to the local fish shop and ordered fish and chips galore. They had money to burn. After a glorious beerup, and listening to their adventures, it was very late when the party packed up. Max went back to the

Sailors' Home somewhere in dockland and was invited to come again tomorrow.

Next morning, I was told not to go to school as I had some errands to do. Bert had quite a bit of money and gave Mum several pounds. I soon discovered what errands I had to get. 'Get the pram and go to the pawnshop,' said Mum. My mother always seemed to have a stack of pawn tickets: she reckoned she could play cards with them. I got the pram and Mum gave me a load of tickets and away I went to McCarthys, a pawnshop in Great Cambridge Street. When I went in with the stack of tickets the chap behind the counter asked me if we had come into a fortune. Anyhow, I got the pram loaded and got them home. There were sheets, costumes, suits and all sorts of goods Mum never knew she had.

Bert said he wasn't home for long and had to see about 'signing on'. Max came during the day and they went to a shipping office to see about their next trip. They came back and said their ship was sailing in about four days, so they were prepared to have a spending spree. During the next four days they painted the Hackney Road red. The old man didn't go to work; he wasn't going to be left out. He was so drunk that he was helpless most of the time. I remember on one occasion he had to be put to bed and he thought he was dying. He was shouting for me in his drunken stupor. I didn't want to go as I had seen him like this before. Mum told me to 'go and see what he wants'. I went in the bedroom and he told me to come nearer and hold his hand. 'Jan, I don't think I'm long for this world,' he said and made me promise to look after my mother. I was the 'only one he could trust' and on and on he went. I stayed with him until he gradually went to sleep, and crept out of the room. I told my mother what he had said and she told me 'not to worry, he'll be about again as soon as the drink wears off'. True enough he was and he didn't remember a thing about it.

Bert and Max went back when the four days were up and promised to be back in six weeks. They were both well and truly broke. So we were back to normal again. Going to Camden Passage for the cloth, putting the stall out on Saturday; nothing had changed. Going to meet Gerry and bringing back the screws and glue. The continual drunken rows at week-ends. I was beginning to wish I was old enough to be able to get away from it all.

I got friendly with a boy who lived at the top end of Scawfell Street, this was the 'upper ten'. No one would play with this boy. All the 'herbs' thought he was a snob. His name was David Pugh. He was Welsh. His father worked in the City and was very strict in the Welsh way of life. One day I was invited to have tea with them. Dave said it was all right as he'd asked his mum. I didn't want to go as I thought it was a bit out of my class. He managed to get me to go in the end. His mother was typically Welsh. I could hardly understand her. He also had two older sisters. I'll never forget sitting down to tea. It was all so different to what I was used to. Luckily I was always taught good manners by my mother and it came in handy on this occasion. I was given the choice of white or brown bread, real butter and jam, cakes and everything. After tea, David and his father asked me out in the garden and we played games. I began to wonder why my father was so different. I didn't know fathers played with their children. Anyhow, although it was out of my class, I enjoyed it and thanked them for having me. I was told I could come again.

Dave and I were always together. We were staunch pals. When we came out of school we used to go for walks to the City. The trouble was I always had to go somewhere or do something. When I had to meet Gerry I used to run all the way to Bethnal Green Road and back. I couldn't tell David what they were up to so I made excuses that I'd be late and would see him later. It was the same when I had to go to my uncle's at Camden Passage.

Dave's family were very religious and were firm supporters of Lloyd George. I didn't mind their politics but could not see eye to eye with their religion. I had seen too much poverty and suffering to have many religious thoughts. We used to argue our points on this but never let it interfere with our friendship. My mother approved of us being friends and on occasions would tell me to bring Dave to tea. We did the best we could, but could not put on a show like Dave's mother. Again, if ever he was at our place, I was always afraid the old man would come in drunk and start his tricks. Dave could play the piano and I was often asked to sing. I had a fair soprano voice as a boy and his family used to encourage me. They liked folk-songs and I didn't go much on them, but it was a change to what I was used to. Looking back now, I am grateful to Dave and his family. Knowing them had a lot to do with my future.

My sister was taken very queer one day; her eyes and face were swollen and she had to go to hospital. She had been painting ammunition boxes and the paint had entered a cut in her finger. She was weeks under the hospital and was not her usual self. She couldn't go to work and Mum missed her money, but she managed somehow. If she had no money there was always the pawnshop. I remember one day I went with Mum to take a parcel to pawn. In front of us, a woman undid a blanket and put it on the counter. 'How much?' said the pawnbroker. 'Two bob,' said the woman. The pawnbroker undid the blanket, punched it several times with his fist and said, 'Go home and take the hops out first.' Poor woman. One laughed at the time about this, but on reflection it only shows the abject poverty that forced this woman to take a blanket off the bed. Some used the pawnshop to get money for food, some for drink. I've seen women take an ordinary flat iron, borrow 3d. on it, get 2½d. after ½d. was stopped for the ticket and go straight to the nearest pub and get a half-qtn. gin. This may seem fantastic in this day and age and if anyone cares to dispute this I can name the pawnshop in Essex Road and the pub. It took all sorts to create the poverty-stricken world we lived in.

It wasn't long before Bert and his mate came home again, six weeks at the most. As soon as they came home the old man refused to go to work. He knew they had plenty of money and he wanted to help them spend it. They were at fault in encouraging him and they would go drinking all day. I was on holiday from school and had the time of my life. Max promised to buy me a new suit. One day he took me to Gardner's

Corner, Whitechapel, and I had the pick of the shop. From there he took me to a restaurant in Cable Street where he seemed to be well known.

He started to take a fancy to my sister Jo', but she didn't go much on him. He was far too old for her, but he was very persistent. She told him time and again that she was going steady with a chap in the Navy. But he still persisted. I remember one night he asked her to go to the pictures. She told him she didn't want to go, and I remember them both looking at each other, they were fed up—Jo' wasn't well at the time, anyway. In the end she said she would go with him, but only if I could go also. Somehow he didn't seem to like this idea, but finally agreed. We walked along the Hackney Road to the Coronet Cinema. When we got there she said she had seen the film and we went home in silence. She would never be alone with him and I had to go along too on more than one occasion.

One day he had to go and sign on for a ship. I went with him to a shipping office and he signed on. Funds were getting low, so he got an advance note. This was issued by the shipping company and was an advance on wages. The note, when issued, could be cashed by the holder at a discount and made payable to the person who cashed it: as soon as the person it was issued to sailed, the value of the note could be claimed from the shipping company. Anyhow, Max went to a Jewish shop in Cable Street, got £4 for the £5 note and took me to the docks to show me his ship. I went on board with him and it was my first experience of a ship. I was astounded at the size of it and wished I was old enough to sail with him. We went back home and in the evening Max suggested they all go for a drink. About eight o'clock he said he had to see about getting away to board his ship. As it was early, someone decided we should go and see him safely aboard. Everyone went, including my young sister and myself. We all got a tram to the docks and went to find the ship. Max asked a chap where the S.S. *Weiwere* was laying. It was pitch-dark and although we had been there in daylight it was hopeless in the dark. We eventually found it and he took his kit aboard. He found out it wasn't going to sail until five o'clock the following morning. Having a few bob left, he decided he had plenty of time to go back home and have a few more drinks. We found out he could get a train early next morning and he would have plenty of time to get aboard by 4 a.m. Needless to say, they all had one over the eight; he overslept and the ship went without him. So now he had no kit, no money and he owed the Jew £4 for defaulting on his advance note. He got out of it by signing on another ship for a longer period in order to get a bigger advance note to clear his debts. Such was the way they carried on.

This was about the time of the Battle of Jutland. Jo' was going steady with a chap on the *Queen Mary*. She had meet him some three years before at Mary's wedding. His name was Charles Mason. Quite a nice chap. One Saturday afternoon his mother came round with a telegram saying he had been killed. Poor Jo', she thought such a lot of him, and she was still very ill and not really strong enough to take the shock. For months afterwards she would visit his mother.

Gerry was getting worried. A Bill was going before

Parliament for Conscription. This meant he would have to go in the army again. He could see no way out of this when his call-up came, so he started to get used to the idea. I know he got a fresh copy of his marriage certificate, making out that it had been lost, because it had been stamped when he had previously joined up. He also started to have nights out. He told Mary he had joined a club and she somehow didn't seem to mind. On Saturday nights he said he was in a billiard game and was playing in a championship. This was supposed to run into several weeks and each week he managed to get into the next round. One Saturday night the old man invited him to a drink at the local. One drink led to another and he never went to his club. Next morning a very nice young lady knocked on the door and asked if Gerry lived here. My sister Jo' answered the door and asked her who she was. 'I'm his young lady,' she said. Jo' called out, 'Mary, Gerry's young lady is here.' Gerry was out, so Mary asked her in and it seemed Gerry had been courting for months and only a week or two before had proposed to her. There was a terrific scene. When she found out Gerry was already married with a child, she asked Mary to forgive her intrusion, but she honestly didn't know. The family could understand her plight and could see she was speaking the truth. The young lady went away terribly disillusioned with all men. When Gerry came in, the fun started. Mary told him she had had a club member round to see her and when he found out what had happened he rushed out of the house, round to the local and got himself well and truly drunk. When he eventually came home, Mary and all the family were waiting on him. There was a terrible fight between him and the old man. He was an old swine, but he certainly put up a show in aid of his daughter. After the fighting had died down Mum gave him a dressing-down. He promised he would never do anything like it again and tried to apologise for all the trouble he had caused.

Mary was still crying when dinner was ready. Gerry picked up a knife to cut the joint, when suddenly he went berserk. He tried to cut his throat but the old man managed to stop him. He somehow got the knife again and managed to cut his wrists. As he drew the knife and the blood flowed, he collapsed. They rushed him to the hospital in Hackney Road. The old man warned him not to say how it happened because they would call the police if they knew it was attempted suicide. So Gerry told them he was cutting the meat and the knife slipped. He came home with his arm in a sling and everyone settled down. At night they went round to the pub, drinking up as though nothing happened. So much for Gerry's club. Although he was never trusted again, I don't think he ever went wrong again with other women.

My brother Bert and his friend Max came home again after a few weeks away and the old routine continued. The old man stayed away from work and was his usual drunken self for three to four days. I remember on this occasion their leave ran into a weekend. The Saturday morning was spent during a round of the pubs and everyone was merry and bright, looking forward to the Saturday night. After something to eat, the old man went to sleep it off. Jo' was feeling very queer and was in bed; she was still swollen round her face and legs. After sleeping it off and having something to eat, the old man, Bert and Gerry went to the local. Mum and Mary promised to see them later. I was looking after my young sister and during the evening Mum and Mary went to have a drink with the crowd.

About nine o'clock I saw the old man stagger round the corner. I don't think I have ever seen him so bad. He evidently knew he was about to be taken short and tried to make it home. He got as far as the scullery and that was his lot. He couldn't make it. I ran upstairs to tell Jo' what had happened and we could smell him. Poor Jo' was feeling sick. He was calling out for me at the top of his voice and I didn't like to go down. Jo' told me to go and she would get up. When I went down he was still calling out but I would not go near him because of the stench. 'Jan,' he said, 'go and tell your mother I've shit myself.' In order to get away from the smell I took to the fresh air and the local. I pushed the bar door open and tried to get Mum's eye. I eventually drew her attention and she came out with Mary. 'What's the matter?' she said. 'The old man told me to tell you he's shit himself,' I said. 'Go back and tell him to bloody well clear it up,' she said. Back I went and there was Jo' on her hands and knees with a bowl of water clearing his mess up. Poor Jo', she was heaving with every breath she took. Mum got back soon after me and stripped the old man and put all his clothes in the copper and made him wash in cold water. What a state to get in. This didn't stop the crowd from coming back and having their party. We never saw anything more of the old man that night.

Next day Jo' was very bad and we had to get the doctor. She must have caught a chill clearing up the night before. The doctor confined her to bed and she must have stayed there for a couple of weeks. When she was well enough to get about she couldn't go back to her old job. I think she got a light job in a sweet factory. I know I used to wait on her coming home at dinner-time. If she could she would bring me sweets, which I used to take to school.

Conscription was eventually introduced and in due course Gerry got his call-up. Worried frantic about his earlier desertion, he went for his medical and was passed A.1. He was eventually sent to Stafford and with a heavy heart he went. He swore he would get out of the army as soon as the opportunity arose.

On one of his short trips, my brother Bert brought another friend home with him and Max. His name was Bertram. He was Irish and one of the best men I have ever met. His family were in business in Dublin and he had had a wonderful education, finishing up at Dublin University. It seemed he would not toe the line at home, his father being very strict. He was a butcher and had a chain of shops in Dublin. Rather than knuckle under to his father he went to America and got various jobs. He had eventually joined the Merchant Navy, and that's how my brother came to meet him. He seemed to get on with my sister Jo', which wasn't to the liking of Max. One wouldn't go out and leave the other one at home if Jo' was there.

Bertram was also older than Jo', but it didn't seem to matter. He didn't seem to drink like the others. They got on so well together that after a second trip they were talking about marriage. This made it awkward for Max. The fact that his friend was doing better with Jo' than he was got under his skin. In any case, Jo' would have nothing to do with him. He was told he didn't stand a chance. When their leave was up they both went to sign on their ships together—at least, that's what Max thought. To our surprise, Bertram was back on the next day. He had not signed on the same ship as Max, but had kidded him he was and had let the ship go with Max alone. His ship sailed that day and he promised that when he came back he and Jo' would get married. The trip was a long one, but he used to write us whenever he could. Max still called on his shorter trips, but knew nothing about my sister's arrangement with Bertram.

Meantime, things were very much the same with us at home. We still had the stall in Hoxton and I was still doing my trips to my uncle's. The old man wasn't doing so well now that Gerry was away and he was looking for other sources of supply. He soon made several contacts so wasn't short of money for long. Mum still managed to go down his pockets when she could, and he never knew. We were beginning to feel the effects of the food shortage now and there was yet another job for me: I had to take out my younger sister, who was now about six years old, to scrounge round the shops. We'd take a bag each and if we saw a queue forming we would line up for two pounds of potatoes. If we could not get potatoes, swedes would have to do: we had to learn to like swedes.

Owing to the air-raids, Mum liked me to be within call and usually I was. I still had my friend Dave, and she thought she could be sure that if I wasn't to be found I must be with him or his parents. One time, however, things didn't work out as usual. I was in the street, early in the morning, waiting for Dave to turn up, when I saw the Cats' Meat Man. He had an enormous round in the district, selling what was known locally as 'rough', that is to say, meat for cats at a ha'penny a time and for dogs at a penny. He would deliver most days and call for the money on Saturday. On this particular day it seemed that his helper had let him down and he asked me if I'd like to stand in and earn a few coppers. This I was always willing to do, so I quickly agreed and off we went. He had a small cart full of meat and a big basket for deliveries; he stayed by the cart, cutting up the meat in small pieces and stuck them on bits of wood, which I delivered from the basket. If people were out I shoved them through the letter-boxes.

It was good fun and when dinner-time came and he took me into a coffee-shop and bought me dinner, sweet and tea, I knew I was on to a good thing and didn't notice that time was getting on. We worked through the afternoon and I was thoroughly enjoying myself. Tea-time arrived, and again he took me somewhere for tea and a cake. I still hadn't realised that Mum must have been wondering where I was, for it hadn't occurred to me to let her know what I was doing. We worked until quite late at night when he thanked me, gave me a shilling and told me to push off home.

I was very pleased with myself as I walked home. I had had a nice day out and was proud of what I had earned, for a shilling was hard enough to come by at the best of times. I got to the corner of our street and was surprised to see quite a crowd outside our house. As I got nearer someone shouted, 'Here he is,' grabbed me and pushed me indoors.

I'll never forget the look on Mum's face when she saw me; she was crying with relief, and when I saw that the old man was sober although it was by now well on the way to closing time I really knew that something must be up.

What was up was that I had been reported to the police as missing. Mum had got worried when I hadn't shown up by dinner-time. She made enquiries from my friends and the neighbours to no avail and by the time the old man got home she was really anxious. They decided they should tell the police and he went down to Old Street Police Station where they took particulars and told him he must bring me to the station to give an explanation if I should turn up. So down to Old Street we all went.

On arrival I was ordered to go in front of the station sergeant; the size of him scared me, but I explained what had happened as best I could. He admonished me for not telling my parents where I was. He made me promise I would never do such a thing again, and we all trooped out. We walked along the Hackney Road slowly while the old man went and got himself a pint. I never went absent again.

Gerry had now been away three months and came home on leave. He was going to France and didn't much like the idea. He still reckoned he would be out of the army as soon as the opportunity presented itself, but this time he wanted a proper discharge; no more being on the run for him.

My elder brother Will came home from New Zealand. We were very proud of him, but somehow he seemed so distant. After being home a few days, he picked up with a girl we had all known for years and seemed to spend more time with her on his leave than with us. She caused a rift between my brother and the family and we hardly saw anything of him during his leave. They eventually got married. None of us went to his wedding. He just was not one of us. My mother never got over his desertion of the family and in future years would not have his name mentioned.

The old man lost his job. Imports of timber were now so small that there was no need to have a salesman. They could sell what they had without him. His next job was in a warehouse in Featherstone Street, just off Old Street. He didn't earn half as much money. But it was his loss rather than ours, for it simply meant he couldn't buy so much drink. The firm he worked for made furniture, brushes and all sorts of domestic woodware and he had to be packing and despatch. We wondered how long it would be before he got involved in some kind of racket. It wasn't long; he started to bring home brushes and brooms, and soon got in the money again.

We were now in 1917 and we were on the move again. Why, I cannot remember. This time we moved to Shepherdess Walk, off City Road. It was a very large house, let off in flats. We had a ground floor and a basement flat consisting of five rooms and scullery. It wasn't a very nice place to live. We moved in the winter, which made matters worse. Food and coal were hard to come by. We all lined up for a seven-pound bag of coal: that's all we were allowed. As soon as I saw a coal-shop selling coal we would all go and line up and get our seven pounds.

During air-raids, if we had time, we all used to go to the Wenlock Brewery in Wenlock Street. It had a basement and crowds used to go. It had hundreds of pipes running all round the walls and if a bomb had dropped on it we would have all drowned. It didn't take the old man long to get in where the beer was concerned. One night he was sitting on the walls of a huge container that had thousands of gallons of beer in it and was all one mass of froth. As it was rising, his coat gradually soaked it up and he smelt like a brewery for weeks. He had a mate who worked there on night work and he often came round with a quart can of beer. He used to sit up after the pubs closed and if the warning went he was first to go down to the brewery basement and the last to leave it.

My brother Bert was now on minesweepers and we hadn't seen him for months. His friend Bertram came home and we were all pleased to see him, especially Jo'. They planned to get married but times were bad. The winter of 1917 was the worst I remember as a child. Bertram wanted to do so much for my sister. He was due back on his ship but decided to miss it. He wouldn't consider going back to sea until he got married. Obviously he had to go in hiding because the police were looking for him (not registering in those days was a crime), so we had to put him up although he had no ration card and we had to manage the best way we could. He knew his father had died and left money so he wrote to a lawyer in Dublin to see how he stood regarding his father's Will. He was informed that his father had provided for him and the lawyer sent him a form to be signed by him and a Commissioner of Oaths. When sent back this would give him an advance of £50 since he was in need, and the settlement would be made at a later date. This was what he had been waiting for. He returned the completed form and to get money quickly he was prepared to borrow. Opposite was a money-lender. He went across to see him and showed him the copy of his father's Will. Being an East End shyster, he saw he was on a good thing. He immediately lent him £20 at an exhorbitant rate of interest, and the wedding took place. It wasn't much of a celebration. Times were too bad and everything was in short supply. The old man managed to get a bottle of whisky and a joint of meat from one of his pals in the market and they made the best of what they could get.

The problem now was for Bertram to get back to sea, but he didn't have the trouble he had anticipated. He just told the authorities he had been living in Ireland. He signed on with the Union Castle Line and was soon away.

We occasionally heard from Gerry in France and somehow he seemed well away from the fighting. He intended it to be this way if he had anything to do with it. But how long could it?

Jo' was still very queer and an appointment was made for her to see a specialist at St. Bartholomew's Hospital. She was beginning to swell all over. Her legs and face were terribly swollen. As soon as the doctor saw her he admitted her straight away. It was a very bad time of the year, about three weeks before Christmas. I remember one wet and foggy Sunday we went to the hospital at the usual visiting time; she seemed fair and the Ward Sister told Mum there was a slight improvement. We were feeling jubilant to think she was getting on at last. But at eleven o'clock that night a policeman knocked on our door to tell us my sister was dangerously ill and wasn't expected to live. My mother and I got dressed and went as fast as we could to the hospital. Mum being on the big side, we couldn't hurry too much. We had to walk to City Road and get a tram to Smithfield Market. At midnight we arrived at the hospital and were shown to the ward where Jo' was. Mum and I were both tear-stained where we had been crying. The nurse showed Mum to Jo's bed. I wasn't allowed in and had to wait in a side ward.

With tears flowing from me, I prayed for my sister the best way I knew. I didn't know much about religion, but I felt I needed it then.

Chapter Five

WE stayed at the hospital until 1 a.m. and were told they would let us know if there was any change and it was pointless to wait any longer. She was managing to hold on to life by a thread. Mum went again on Monday and it seemed that my prayers had been answered. She had passed the critical period and every hope was now given for a recovery. We were all overjoyed with the news. I was especially happy, for I loved her very much. She had always been so good to me. She was thought sufficiently recovered to be allowed to come home about a week before Christmas. She still looked very ill and was told to take things easy, which Mum saw that she did.

This was a very bad time for Mum. We no longer had the stall in Hoxton, because we couldn't buy anything to sell. The old man was still the same, drinking what he could get and not caring two hoots about us. Jo' had no allowance from Bertram yet, and it was a hand-to-mouth existence. Gerry came home on leave from France; he didn't look much the worse for his experiences of the war, but he had no spare cash.

One day I had to run for the doctor. I had just come out of school and Mary was groaning in agony. The doctor came and Mary had to go to hospital immediately. The ambulance came and took her to Charing Cross Hospital and they operated on her immediately.

We were now well and truly in trouble. Jo' was still very queer and Mum had Mary's baby to look after. All this happened two days before Christmas. I knew we couldn't get anything for Christmas dinner in the shops. Mum managed to get round the old man to see one of his mates in the meat market. All he could get was a big breast of mutton and told her she was 'bleeding lucky to get that'. It wasn't a very happy Christmas.

Mary asked Mum to bring me up to see her after dinner on Christmas Day. They were having a party in the ward and tea afterwards. Mum couldn't go because of the baby and Jo' so I went with Gerry. It was a nice party. All the stars of the day showed up. One I remember in particular was Ella Shields. We all had to sing songs that were popular during the war. This was followed by a grand tea. Mary told me to eat all I could get, which I did. We arrived home about eight o'clock. Mum was nursing the baby who never seemed to stop crying. Gerry and the old man went for a drink, and stayed out until closing time, giving no thought for my mother.

We were glad to get that Christmas over. It is one of the worst in my memory.

Mary came home after two weeks and things began to settle down again.

Jo' was gradually getting better, but she found out that she was pregnant. This didn't improve her health. How, after what she had been through, she could ever manage to have a baby, nobody could see. The amazing thing was that she was improving.

We still owed the rent man. Every Monday he would knock and nearly every Monday he was told, 'We'll bring it up during the week.' Sometimes we did: most times we didn't. Consequently we were running into long arrears. I had an idea we would soon be on the move again.

We weren't alone with this thought. Next door lived a very large family. The mother and father used to go out with a horse and van and collect rags and any old junk they could get. They would unload and bring everything inside the house and all would have to work sorting the rags and breaking up the old furniture. Next morning the eldest son would take the broken furniture round to the stables and chop it up for firewood and sell it round the streets. They owed everyone. Eventually they got orders to 'Get out' and had to go. The house stood empty for some time.

Empty houses always held a fascination for us, as children, and if we could get in an empty house and play 'Mothers and Fathers' it was our delight. Usually I would play the drunken husband; I had plenty of knowledge on this sort of character. Some girl would be mother and all the smaller kids would be our children. I would come home and want to know why the dinner wasn't ready and start to clump the kids and be the tyrant father. After the game we would rummage through the house and try to imagine how and what the last tenants did. I wandered in the basement one day and saw six chairs. They looked in wonderful condition and I told Mum what I had discovered. 'Let me have a look at one,' she said. Back I went next door and got one. 'They look all right,' says Mum, 'are they all like that?' 'Yes,' I said. She decided we would have them. I got the six chairs on the garden wall and Mum took them from me. We decided to put them under the stairs in the basement for the time being.

That night we had an air-raid. We were too late to go to the Wenlock Brewery shelter, so we thought the safest place for us would be under the stairs. We set the chairs out so we could all sit down. We hadn't sat down long before one or two of us started to scratch ourselves. Soon we were all scratching. We just couldn't make out why. Suddenly Mum reckoned it was the chairs. Amid the gunfire we threw them out in the garden. They were alive with fleas. When the air-raid was over we had to shake our clothes and wash.

Next day Mum sent me for a pint of paraffin and I burned them. We should have known better than to have had them in the first place. The next-door people being rag-totters we might have known they were 'alivo'. I was not allowed in the house again.

While on the subject of air-raids, I remember one Saturday morning when we had one of the worst raids of the war. Without any warning, German aeroplanes were dropping bombs all around us. The old man was home from work with the gout. On this particular occasion he was in bed with his leg up on a pillow. In those days it was a regular thing to have a 'jerry' under the bed. As the bombs were dropping, the old man goes to make a quick move to get under the stairs and knocks his tobacco box into the 'jerry'. He roared and created about the 'bastard Germans'. 'All me bleeding bacca's gone,' he said. 'Serves you bloody well right,' says Mum. 'You shouldn't have the jerry under the bed, especially in the day time.' 'You don't expect me to go to the bleeding closet with a foot like this,' the old man retorted. And that's how it went on all through the raid.

My brother's friend, Max, came home again and stayed with us during the two to three days his ship was in port. He was disappointed to find my sister Jo' was married, especially to someone whom he had introduced. He spent his money like water. We always had a royal time when Max was home. It was about this time we discovered that he was a bit of a sharp boy. Just before he was due back he lost all his money gambling. This particular day he went out about three o'clock in the afternoon and said he would be back later. About eight o'clock he came back with a Polish seaman named Silonski. He introduced him as a friend of long-standing. They brought in loads of fish and chips, bottles of beer and some rum for the old man. We couldn't understand a word this chap said. Max was the only one who could make him understand. He spoke several languages. Everyone was sitting round the table eating and drinking and the old man was well drunk and getting insulting. As he got up from the table he was rolling and he accused my mother of having an affair with Max. This was the only time I have ever been near to seeing a murder committed. Max got up and laid into the old man and nearly choked him to death. Everyone had to pull him off. The old man was going blue in the face. It was terrible. They carried him into the bedroom and he gradually came round. There was nothing that a drop of rum wouldn't do for my father. About eleven o'clock Max told Silonski it was time to go. He shook hands all round and away they went. Max was back about twelve o'clock with a roll of notes. He had evidently robbed Silonski and left him stranded. Max went away next day and we never saw him again. He must have got torpedoed and lost his life, for he would always come to see us when his ship docked.

My friend Dave from Scawfell Street kept in touch with me and still used to invite me back to his home. They were very kind people but I always felt out of place. My clothes were always so shabby in comparison with Dave's. They used to invite me chiefly to sing. I didn't mind; there was always a good spread to eat.

Jo's time to have her baby was getting near. She was supposed to go to the Lying-in-Hospital in Old Street, but Mum wouldn't let her go owing to the air-raids.

Mary had heard from the War Office that Gerry had been wounded. Afterwards the official letter said he was suffering from shell-shock and was on his way home. This worried us all because we had seen some of the lads suffering from this. They used to shake from head to foot and had to be assisted in anything they did. He eventually arrived and Mary went to see him. When she came home from the hospital she said his condition was fair. It was only his head that was shaking and as soon as he showed some improvement he would be allowed home for a few hours. One Sunday afternoon, some weeks after Mary had visited him, he came home for a few hours. He had hospital-blue uniform and a stick. He had got ever so fat. We were all pleased to see him. He had a slight shake of his head. The peculiar thing was it only shook sometimes;

when he was interested in anything he seemed to be quite normal. The old man noticed this and decided he 'had no bleeding shell-shock—it's a put-up job to get out of the bloody army'. He waited for him to leave before he said this, but I must admit the old man seemed right.

Jo' had her baby. It was a little girl. A sweet little thing and we called her Flossie.

We now needed more room. So it was on the move again, when Jo' was well enough. Mum, Mary and Jo' wanted a house where we could all live together with plenty of room. They saw one in Bridport Place—No. 41. It was a large flat-fronted house with two storeys above ground floor. How they ever managed to get such a place I don't know. The landlords must have been glad to let houses to anyone. If references had been required we could never produce one. We were now back to where my story first started. We had to get a horse and van to move with. Mary had the ground floor, Jo' the first floor, we had the top floor and the old man had his favourite pub, the Bridport Arms. I knew the area well and we knew most of the people around.

Gerry got his ticket from the army with a pension. I don't think it was much. He got his job back in Bethnal Green, and he and the old man were considering going back again into the glue and screw racket. I would not have anything to do with it this time and told my mother I didn't want to. She told them in no uncertain terms where to get off and Gerry had to manage with what he could bring home at nights.

I did get involved in a glue racket my father started

on his own, but I was unsuspecting. He asked me one day to meet him at dinner-time with a barrow: this was on a Saturday. As soon as my mother knew, she refused to let me go. 'It's nothing pinched,' he said. 'It's only a sack of firewood I want him to take to someone.' Believing him she let me go. I took the barrow to Featherstone Street, Old Street, and the firm was shut. I waited outside a few minutes and the gate shutters were pulled up enough for me to go in. The old man and another chap humped a huge sack on the barrow and told me to take it to Brick Lane where he would meet me. I stopped under the arch at Great Eastern Street for a rest. I looked at the sack and thought I had never seen firewood in such accurate shapes. I undid the string stitching at the corner of the sack and saw it was cakes of Scotch glue. I knew I had been taken in. When the old man arrived I told him what I had discovered and I intended to tell my mother when I got home. I was getting old enough now to talk to him. He knew I had not wanted to help him pinch things; I was seeing too many of my school-mates being put away for thieving for me to want to do anything like that. He begged me not to split on him. 'Don't tell your mother and I'll give you half a crown,' he said. Never having had half a crown, I accepted. When he unloaded the glue he gave me two and six, and made me promise not to tell. 'I might want you to come again next week,' he said and the half-crown came to my mind. I said I would go. When I got home I told Mum I got two and six from the man I took the firewood to. I gave her one and six and went to the pictures that night.

Opposite the house was a small general shop. They

sold groceries and at the back was a large shed. The chap who owned the shop was a cabinet-maker and he worked in the shed while his wife ran the shop. I often used to go and watch him at work. He told me he just could not get glue and asked me if I knew where any could be got. 'If you can get any, Jan, I would give you two and six a pound for it.' They were his words and I began to think. I found myself a small sack and looked forward to next Saturday.

The following Friday night the old man asked me to come to the usual place with a barrow. I told him I would get the sack unloaded at the shop where he took it last week as I was in a hurry to get back. He said that would be O.K. and he would see me when he got back. I got the barrow loaded and was on my way. I had a stop at the usual place, under the railway arch at Great Eastern Street, and started to undo the stitching on the sack. I took out eight cakes of glue and put them in my own bag. I then delivered the glue and was off home. Before going home I took my bag into the grocer's shop and told the lady I had managed to get her husband his glue. She called him out and he was delighted. He weighed it and he gave me ten shillings. I went home and told my mother what I had done. She was annoyed to think I had gone against her wishes. I gave her seven and sixpence and told her there was no risk. In any case, it was the old man's responsibility. I was only doing as I was told.

I had never had the fantastic sum of five shillings in my pocket. I was very sweet on a girl who lived opposite. Her name was Mary and we used to meet when we came out of school and walked home together. She invited me to her home on one or two occasions. Her father was crippled, as a result of the war, and her mother used to make hand-made cigarettes at home. It was through her I learned to smoke. Mary would often give me a few cigarettes and I would smoke them on the quiet. Anyhow, with five shillings in my pocket I thought I would give Mary a night out. I asked her mother if I could take her to the Olympia in Shoreditch. She gave me permission and we had two seats in the pit. This, plus sweets and fruit, soon made a hole in my five shillings. I didn't mind though; she was a nice girl and worth it. We saw a revue called *The Byng Boys are Here*. We did this outing on two or three occasions when I could get the money.

To help out at home, I got myself a job after school hours at a small printers. I was learning to work a Platen printing machine. I got four and six a week, and had to work from five o'clock till eight o'clock and Saturday mornings. The August holidays came around and I was offered a full month's work. Ten shillings a week, eight o'clock to six o'clock. I readily agreed and started on Monday morning of the first week of the holidays. Being opposite the house, I was told I could go home for morning tea. I went home at ten-thirty and was just drinking my tea when Bertram, my sister Jo's husband, walked in from sea.

We hadn't heard from him in months. He went crazy when he saw his baby. She was lovely and he was like a little boy with a new toy. He undone his kitbag and he brought out sugar, tea, tins of milk, ham and all foodstuffs we couldn't buy. I was proud to tell him I was working during my school holidays. He told me I shouldn't do it as I would have enough work when I left school. When I told him we needed the money he told me not to worry, he would see to that. He had to go back to the docks to get paid off and asked me to go with him. I went to tell the printer I wouldn't be back any more and he wasn't too pleased: he had lost a good bargain. Sixty hours work for ten shillings. I wasn't worried about him though; I was looking forward to going with my brother-in-law.

After dinner we went and he took me over the ship. It was a Union Castle ship called the *Galway Castle*. I was amazed at the size of it. I began to wish I was old enough to sign on. After about an hour he had to go to the office to get paid off. He came out with a stack of pound-notes. I had never seen so much money. We went into a restaurant and he told me to have just what I wanted. He gave me a royal time. When we got home he gave my sister most of his money and gave me the £2 which I would have earned if I had gone to work. I gave most of this to Mum, who promised she would put it towards a new suit she had promised me. It was a long time since I had had a suit, and was looking forward to it. I got it eventually and Mum promised it wouldn't go to Pawn. I was so used to wearing 'hand me downs' that I couldn't believe it.

Bertram told us he would only be home until the Thursday. As he only had three more days leave, he intended to live it up. At night he asked Gerry (who had somehow made a marvellous recovery), the old man and all who cared to go for a 'booze-up' at the Bridport. It must have seemed like old times at the Bridport Arms for the old man and the family to be back. They all had a right royal time and brought back plenty of drink. This was usual at the time. Anyone who came home on leave always had a beer-up. We still had a gramophone and they nearly danced the floor in.

Gerry and the old man were soon at it again. They just could not agree when they had been drinking. There was the usual fight between the two of them and Gerry got the shakes. He went berserk, opened the window and was going to jump out. My sisters screamed and managed to hold him back after much struggling. I was standing outside and saw the window go up amid a lot of shouting and screaming, but I have often wondered since if he would really have jumped. When the old man saw him open the window and attempt to jump he is supposed to have said, 'Let him bleeding well jump and good riddance.' They got Gerry to bed and had to send for a doctor. All the doctor told him was to lay off the drink as it was aggravating his complaint.

There was no work for anyone next morning. When Gerry and the old man met they just glared at each other. Peace was made by an invitation by Bertram for 'a quiet one at the Bridport'. By one o'clock they were all good pals again.

Bertram's three days soon went and amid many tears he went back. Mum thought the world of him and she was heartbroken to see him go.

Mum was getting sick of the old man and Gerry fighting and rowing every week-end when they had been drinking and suggested to Mary that they should find a place of their own. It wasn't much of a life for anyone and she agreed to move if she could. My girl-friend who lived opposite happened to mention to me one day that a flat was empty in the house where she lived. I told Mary and she went across to have a look at it. She decided to take it and I was pleased because this gave me an opportunity to see more of my girl. About September 1918, Mary moved and we were now left with a house that was too big for us, so Mum and Jo' started to look around for another place. They found a six-roomed flat over a dairy in New North Road, and we moved again. I have never heard of a family who moved more than we did; perhaps we must have had a gipsy trait in us somewhere.

We now lived in a very nice place in the main road. The rooms were large and there was always something going on. Jo' had two rooms, we had the other four. The old man was still working at the same place and still keeping my mother short of money. She was now taking in dressmaking. This meant she was on the machine from morning till night. The old man still came home every night and week-ends the worse for drink. It still wasn't very pleasant, but the war was getting towards the end and we were hoping for better things.

One Saturday afternoon, we were all having tea when a telegram arrived for Jo'. It was from the Union Castle Shipping Line, telling her that the *Galway Castle* had been torpedoed and there were fears for the safety of her husband. We couldn't believe we would never see Bertram again. We tried all ways to kid Jo' that he must have been saved. She wouldn't have it. We got an evening paper and it was all over the front page. The paper said only a few survivors. We tried to tell Jo' that he might be among them. During the week, we had confirmation that he had been missing and was now presumed dead. We managed to get the address of one of the survivors and my father and I went to see him in order to comfort my sister. The chap knew Bertram and said he was on watch at the time the ship was torpedoed and didn't stand a chance. So my sister, a bride of a few months, was left a widow with little Flossie. She was given a pension and £300 was granted by the shipping company as compensation. This had to be drawn when she was in need, at the discretion of the Court.

Armistice was declared on November 11th and the worst war in history was over. People were going mad with joy. The streets were packed with men and women singing and dancing and the pubs sold out of beer, much to my father's disgust. While all this celebration was going on, poor Jo' was sitting at the window, with little Flossie on her lap, crying. We couldn't do much with her. Mum told me to go round to Mary and see if she and Gerry would come around. When Mary saw the state Jo' was in she suggested we all go out. Gerry reckoned it would be a good plan to go to Homerton and see his mother and father. It would get Jo' out, so we all got ready and got the bus to Homerton. The old man wouldn't come. He was in pursuit of any pub that had beer. Gerry's mum was glad to see us all. She got something to eat and Gerry and his father got some drink from somewhere and they celebrated the end of the war in their own way. Gerry found a shop that was selling fireworks and he bought me some. Half of them were duds. They had been in stock since 1913. As the time went on, Jo' gradually got used to the idea of never seeing Bertram again, and settled down.

The war had robbed the district of many familiar people, but one of those who came back was 'Uncle George'. Uncle George was the husband of one of my mother's friends, Annie South. Uncle George was a rag-and-bone man and they had a pretty drab existence. Many is the time on a Monday morning when he would knock on our door and ask Mum if she could 'lend him a start'. This meant that he wanted to borrow a shilling as capital for his day's trading. If she had one to lend, he always got it and always paid her back as soon as he had bought and sold enough rags. He was in the Reserves and I remember him coming to kiss us goodbye in 1914. A few months later he came back minus a leg. Somehow he did not seem to mind: at least, he and his family would never starve again. His pension would see to that.

This was my last year at school and I was very big for my age. I tried to get myself a job after school hours, and eventually found one. I was passing a big old house when I happened to see a board outside with the name and stating they were artificial-flower manufacturers. I knocked and went in and asked if they wanted a boy to make himself useful after school. When the governor saw how big I was he offered me a job cutting out leaves for the flowers at four shillings a week. I accepted and soon learned the ropes. I had to stand at a bench which had a huge square of lead 18 inches by 18 inches by 4 inches. Some green shiny material was folded into six thicknesses. A steel stamp cut out the leaves when I whacked it with a seven-pound hammer. I did this from five o'clock until eight o'clock each evening and I knew I had been working. I stuck it out, though, and the few bob came in handy at home.

My brother Bert came home from the Far East. He had been minesweeping. He didn't stay home long. He found himself a girl-friend and went to stay with her people. This was all right while his money lasted, but when he was broke, back he came. He couldn't settle down. He just had to have discipline. He tried many jobs but couldn't keep one longer than a week.

Mum had a lot to put up with. Things should have been better for her now we were nearly all grown up, but it didn't work out that way for her. There was always a problem of some sort that held her back. Bert was ill for a long time. He had caught some sort of tropical disease out East and was attending hospital.

Now yet another problem was in store for Mum. One Sunday afternoon Jo' took her baby to see some friends. She was in black at the time and it didn't take passers-by long to see she was a widow. On the way home, as she was waiting for the bus at Old Street Station, a chap came up and asked her if he could help her with the baby. He was in the Royal Naval Air Service and looked very smart. He saw my sister home and she asked my mother if she could bring him in. Mum told her she was her own mistress and could do as she liked. She brought him in and they seemed to take to one another straight away. His name was Arthur and he was expecting his demob very soon. He called again next day, and did so regularly for a week or two.

It seems he had been married before but was now divorced. They decided to settle down and get married as soon as he was demobbed. This started the family talking. One reckoned she should be ashamed of herself so soon after Bertram's death. Mum wouldn't get involved. She told her she hoped she knew what she was doing: what did she know about him? Nothing. What had caused the divorce and who was to blame? All these things came up but it was no use, Jo' had made up her mind. Mum tried to tell her to wait a bit longer but it was no use. The old man made it plain that he didn't like Arthur, but nobody took any notice of him—he didn't like anybody.

When Arthur got demobbed they got married and came to live with us. We thought we had the Duke of Wapping living with us. He did fancy his weight. He dressed in Harris-tweed suits, walking stick, felt velour hat; he had the lot. 'Who the bleeding hell does he think he is?' the old man would say. He would ignore me and my young sister Molly. He'd pass us on the stairs without a remark. Gerry couldn't stand him. Mary wouldn't speak to him. She said she felt awkward when he spoke to her. Nobody in the family could get on with him. If anyone complained to my mother about him ignoring us she would tell us to take no notice. Any complaint to Jo' fell on deaf ears. She wouldn't have a word said against him. He was just self-centred and thought we were all beneath him.

He used to take Jo' to the West End and we would have little Flossie to look after until they came home.

We began to notice that Jo' was always short of money. She started to go to the Court to get a grant from the £300 the shipping company had put in trust for her. Arthur was back at his old job on the Railway as a ticket collector. He still ignored us; he would come home and hardly show his face. He never spoke of the past and no mention was ever made of his former wife.

One day we had another shock. Mr. Marshall, who owned the dairy downstairs, came up and asked to see the old man. He and Gerry were discussing who was going to win the Derby. Gerry thought Panther would win and the old man couldn't see anything to beat Lord Glanelly's Grand Parade. This was the first post-war Derby and whenever these two met arguments and discussions on the merits of horses always seemed to be the topic of the day. I broke up the discussion by telling the old man Mr. Marshall wanted to see him. He told me to ask him in. He shocked us by saying he was going to sell the dairy and we would have to quit the flat. He told us he had a house at Walthamstow we could rent and he would pay all the expenses if we would move.

In 1919 Walthamstow to us was like moving to the country. The whole family discussed the matter and it was agreed they would go and see the place. The old man was against going. Jo' didn't like the idea because of the distance from Arthur's work. After seeing the house nobody thought much of it and conveyed their feelings to Mr. Marshall. He explained that he had offered us alternative accommodation. If we didn't go he would have no alternative but to take us to Court to get us out.

Places to live in were now getting harder to get. So under the circumstances it looked as though we were on our way.

Chapter Six

WE moved to Walthamstow in the first week of July 1919. It was a small house just off the High Street. The rent was eight shillings per week. Jo' and Arthur came with us and had to manage in one room. There were five of us and we needed the rest of the house. Arthur had to get a transfer to Manor House Station. This journey he did by cycle every day. The old man had to go to Liverpool Street every day and swore and cursed about the journey. He used to catch the six-thirty workman's train each morning. The fare was twopence return. I had three weeks to go before I was fourteen, and thought I could start work without going to another school. This I was not allowed to do, and had to finish my time at Pretoria Avenue School. I was mad about this but try as I might I had to go until my birthday came. I was anxious to start work. I tried working in a grocer's shop, but didn't like it. I wanted to do something more constructive, and where I could get the most money.

The old man said he would put a word in for me at his place, and one night he came home and told me he had spoken to the Mill foreman and I was to go next morning for an interview at ten o'clock. I got up early and caught the six-thirty with my old man. I went with him to a coffee-shop and had something to eat. He started at eight o'clock, so I had two hours to waste. I walked about some of my old haunts in Hoxton and was outside the office at ten prompt. I was told to start next day. My wage was to be £1 a week. I didn't expect so much money and was delighted to think I would be able to help out at home. I told Mum the good news and it was arranged I should have six shillings and Mum fourteen. This seemed a fair arrangement to me.

I started work next morning and from there I learned my trade as a wood-working machinist and cabinet-maker. It was all very strange at first. The noise on entering the sawmills was deafening and I didn't think I would stick the day out. But I soon got used to it.

Things were now better at home for my mother. My bit of money was regular and with the bit of dress-making she was doing she managed to get by.

I was beginning to like our new surroundings. For a penny you could get into Epping Forest, and this was all so different to the slums of Hoxton and Bethnal Green. My friend Dave would come some week-ends and we had some good times together in the forest.

With Jo', however, things were plainly not going at all well, and Mum took her aside and asked her what the trouble was. Mum could see that she had started to pawn things and that her compensation money had run out. She said she just could not manage on Arthur's money. She said she couldn't ask him to give her more, but Mum made her have a showdown. He soon knuckled down, but now he was more in his shell than ever. He still continued to ignore everybody. Jo' was now beginning to see where she had gone wrong. They had a terrible row and in the end she told him to go. He went out and then he came back for his things. She packed his case, threw it out of an upper window and away he went. About two hours later he crept back and they had a reconciliation, on her terms. Looking back now, I suppose there wasn't much else she could do with the baby coming. He toed the line afterwards and Jo's word was law. He never attempted to hold back money from her again and, in the end, we all got to know each other better.

The old man was still getting his drink. I used to come back on the same train as him on leaving work, but he would always get out at St. James Street Station and go straight to his local, the Cock Tavern in the High Street. Soon he got into the habit of taking days off. The ranks of the unemployed were swelling and Mum used to tell him that one day he would get the sack. True enough he did. He came home one Friday night and said he had got put off. This wasn't going to make any difference to my mother regarding money, so she didn't worry too much. He used to go out at eleven o'clock in the morning, come home at three o'clock, sleep during the afternoon and go out again at six o'clock until ten oclock. All the money he got from the Labour Exchange he kept and spent on beer.

To raise an extra few shillings, he took on the job of runner to a local bookmaker. He would stand outside the Cock and between pints would collect bets. He and his pals had taken a brick out of the wall in the Gent's lavatory at the side of the pub and every half-hour the old man would go out to the lavatory, take out the loose brick, put the bets in the recess and replace the brick. The bookmaker would call at regular intervals, collect the bets and be away. The cash was paid in when the pub closed. This was done in case the old man got picked up by the police. He was questioned several times but nothing was ever found on him to prove he had been taking bets. One day, though, he did get done. He was paying out two old women and there was an argument about threepence. He wouldn't have it that they were right and, to prove his point, started to reckon the bet up. During the argument, unbeknown to him, a plain-clothes policeman had been listening and watching, for he had been suspected for some time. As he showed the old ladies his piece of paper with the bet reckoned up, the policeman came and grabbed him. He had to appear at Stratford and got fined £5. He had no time for old women after that.

About December 1920 I had a bad bout of bronchitis. My mother took me to St. Bartholomew's Hospital and after examination I was told to give up my job in the sawmills as the wood dust would ruin me. This was a blow as I was the only one at work in my family, but my mother insisted that I must give the job up. I tried hard to get an outdoor job, but there were about two million unemployed and it was impossible to get any sort of job. I wasn't old enough for sickness or unemployment benefit and things were pretty grim. The old man had run out of his unemployment benefit and was on public relief. The Relieving Office gave him eight shillings in money for the rent and the rest in food tickets which hardly enabled us to exist. Mum was trying to get me new-laid eggs for my chest, which she used to heat up in milk. I know she used to go without herself to give me eggs and milk. My brother Bert was only getting fifteen shillings on the Labour Exchange. The old man used to keep the eight shillings and give Mum the food tickets. I was earning nothing. Nearly everyone we knew was in similar circumstances.

About three weeks before Christmas 1921 Mum had a letter from Mary saying Gerry was out of work and they were having a rough time. Could they come and stay with us for Christmas? Mum and Jo' talked it over and asked them to come about ten days beforehand. I had to give up my bed, so did my brother, and at night we made a bed up on the floor. Mum was determined to give us all a good Christmas. Weeks before, she made up frocks and trousers out of anything she could lay her hands on. A week before Christmas she found a space for a small barrow in the High Street market and sold most of the things she had made up.

Meanwhile, Gerry hadn't been idle. He had seen an advertisement for cheap Christmas cards and reckoned if he could borrow the money to buy a couple of hundred he would do all right. He asked Mum and, always a soft touch, she lent him £1, which was a fortune to her, telling him if he lost it in the venture there would be no Christmas dinner. He bought the cards, went and got some old wooden boxes, and made himself a stall and stood in the High Street. I must hand it to Gerry that he wasn't lazy. Someone lent him a tarpaulin to make a cover and he was well set. The first three days he sold out. He'd made a fair profit and took a chance and bought four hundred cards. He only had four days in which to sell them. One of these four days disaster nearly caught him. The wind was blowing a gale and Mary asked me to take him a jug of tea and some sandwiches. Just as I got there a gust of wind blew his stall up in the air and landed in the middle of the road. Poor Gerry, the look of despair on his face as the Christmas cards were blowing all up the High Street. We managed to salvage most of them. Luckily it wasn't raining. In the end he succeeded in selling all his cards at a good profit; he paid Mum back and was well set for a good Christmas.

By night-time on Christmas Eve, everyone was set for a good session at the Cock Tavern in the High Street. There was Gerry, the old man and my brother Bert. Mum, Jo' and Mary and the children were at home getting everything ready for Christmas. About ten-thirty the trio came home, loaded with drink inside and out. They had a gallon jar each and several bottles.

According to Bert they had been in a fight. Evidently someone was taking it out on the old man, an argument developed and a fight started. By all accounts they must have got the advantage as they were all merry and bright. Arthur was on late turn on the Railway and when he got in they welcomed him with a drink. To everyone's amazement, he took it. As they were all drinking up and singing, there was a loud knock on the door. I opened up and a huge chap was standing there with a notebook. He asked for the old man by name. I went and told him he was wanted. 'Who the hell wants me on Christmas Eve?' he said. 'Go and see,' I told him. He went to the door and this chap told him he was a detective-inspector, looking into the fight that had taken place previously. Everyone went out in the street and a right argument took place.

As they were arguing, a small stocky chap and his wife were passing the door and heard the argument. He stopped and listened and heard the so-called detective ask them all to accompany him to the station. 'Ask him for his warrant,' said the stranger. 'Yes,' said Gerry, 'I never thought of that—where *is* your warrant?' The detective stands under the street lamp and starts trying to find the warrant, which he never had. By now the stranger feels really involved. 'You're no bleeding tec,' he says and gives him a real right-hander straight to the chin. Down goes the detective, knocked out cold. 'Good night all,' said the stranger, and away he went, leaving his wife behind. She told us he was a boxer and a real terror. From round the corner four or five people came running and saw the 'detective' lying in the road. They explained to Jo' that he wasn't a real detective but just a friend of one of the people who had got the worst of the fight trying to frighten Gerry and the old man into believing he was.

In the end, the tec recovered, everyone went inside and made it up, apologised and departed the best of friends: all promised to see each other at the Cock on Christmas morning. And they did. That was typical of Gerry and the old man. If they weren't fighting each other, they'd fight someone else.

The following evening all got together for a real beer-up. Where the old man had found the money, I just don't know. During the evening everyone wanted to know where Arthur was. Jo' said he wouldn't come down. He had a row with the old man previously and would only come down if the old man apologised; he was like that. He thought there was only one person right in this world and that was him. In order to keep the peace and get the party going, the old man went up and apologised to Arthur. It was one of the few occasions I ever felt sorry for him, as I knew what it must have meant for his pride. Arthur came down in the end and everyone got going.

Christmas ended, and, to everyone's surprise, no more fights. The day after Boxing Day, Mary and Gerry went home and we got back to normal.

Nothing much happened during the first two or three months of 1922. My health improved and I was feeling much better. I still could not get employment of any kind. About March things became desperate at home. We were living below subsistence level but the old man was still somehow managing to get enough money to buy drink with. Mum became suspicious that perhaps he was using the rent money. He was supposed to pay the rent every Friday afternoon when he got the money from the Relieving Office. She hadn't seen the rent book for weeks and when she approached him about it he would say they kept the book at the rent office. One day Mum asked me to look around the bedroom to see if he had hidden it anywhere. I looked in every conceivable place but couldn't find it anywhere. I was on the point of giving up when suddenly I noticed a crack in the corner of the lino. I lifted it up and there was the rent book. When we checked up, he hadn't paid for eight weeks.

When he came home after three o'clock there was one almighty row. How could he have done such a thing? My poor mother had to rake around and get a few things together to try and make a parcel to pawn in order to get a couple of weeks' rent so that we could save ourselves from getting notice to quit. Mum and Jo' managed to raise enough for two or three weeks' rent between them and Jo' took it to the rent office and explained what my father had done. They told her we would have got notice to quit long beforehand but that they had felt so sorry for him that they had put it off. He was never trusted to pay the rent after that.

By now I was about sixteen and a half, and I decided that it would be best for all if I were to try to join the army, so I went to Whitehall and asked to join the Royal Garrison Artillery. I had a medical but was told to come back after a rest. I went and sat outside for an hour and went back again. After another examination I was duly accepted, given a day's pay and told to call every day until my references had come through.

When I got home and told Mum what I had done she burst into tears and asked me why I had to do such a thing. I gave her my reason but she didn't see my point of view. I went to Whitehall every day for three days and each morning my mother used to see me off at the door crying. I was duly accepted and went to Woolwich for training. This wasn't so bad, as I managed to get home most week-ends. I got eighteen shillings per week and made an order to Mum for five shillings a week. This was a great help to her. She still had my young sister Molly at home but somehow she got by.

After being stationed at Woolwich for three months I was sent for gunnery training at Southsea. After passing out, I was put on draft to Malta and given a month's leave. During this leave I could see things getting worse at home. The old man's dole had been stopped and he had to work on public relief work to earn his relief. This didn't amount to much and by the time he had his share Mum was left with almost nothing.

Much as I liked being in the army, I knew that, as I was still under seventeen, I could get out on compassionate grounds if I could find someone prepared to employ me. I tackled the milkman who had a one-man business and asked him if he would give me a job if I got out of the army. After a lot of discussion he promised me a job at thirty-five shillings per week. I told Mum what I intended to do and she was delighted. I told her and Jo' that when my leave was finished and I returned to Southsea they were to write to my Commanding Officer, explaining I was barely seventeen and asking them to discharge me on the grounds of my age and the fact that I was wanted to help keep our home together by taking the job I was offered.

A week after my return to barracks, I was called into the Company Office and told by my Commanding Officer that they had received a letter from my mother. After asking me about conditions at home, he was very sympathetic and told me I would be recommended for discharge, but I would have to wait a little. Meanwhile I was to be taken off the Malta draft and given a job as storekeeper.

One morning I received a letter from my sister Jo'

telling me little Flossie had passed away. I was stricken with grief and couldn't believe it. She had grown into a beautiful child and it just didn't seem possible. I showed the letter to my sergeant, who immediately granted me ten days leave. I got home as soon as I could and the house was like a morgue. Even the old man was upset. It seemed that little Flossie had got diphtheria and this was only discovered when it was too late to save her.

We got as much money together as we could and started to make arrangements for the funeral. Gerry and Mary were staying with us at the time. They bought what black they could afford and Mary suggested dyeing several articles black. So she and Jo' got a bath of water and started dyeing. When they were nearly through it was discovered the old man never had any black trousers, so I gave him a pair of khaki slacks, which Mary and Jo' promptly started to dye black. As they had already used up most of the power of the dye, the trousers became only dark green. To make them black Mary suggested putting soot in the water, which she did. They had to let it go at that and they were duly dried and pressed.

It was a sad day when we buried little Flossie; we just could not believe we would never have her with us again. After the service, we were coming home in the coach when a watery sun started to shine through the window. It settled on the old man's trousers. Sad as the occasion was, we somehow had to laugh. The sun brought out the colour in his trousers and black and green patches appeared. As soon as Mary saw them she winked at Jo' and pointed to the trousers. Remembering the caper they had cut when they were doing the dyeing, they both found it hard to keep back their giggles. I will say this for my family, however sad the occasion there was always someone who would try to raise a laugh.

I duly returned from leave and was given my discharge in December 1922. Mum and Jo' were glad I was home and hoped I would settle down. My first move was to the milkman who promised me a job. He was sorry, he said, but things were bad and he couldn't see his way clear to employ me. So now I was back where I started. I just did not know where to turn for a job. Christmas was a week or so away and it looked like being another grim one. As usual, Mum had made up a load of frocks and coats and sold them in the High Street which got us our Christmas.

After Christmas things were worse than ever. If I could get twopence I would walk to Shoreditch and Bethnal Green, and try all the cabinet-making dives in the East End. After doing the rounds, I would get a tram back to Walthamstow for twopence. But it seemed hopeless and I would have done better to stay at home and save my boot-leather.

From 1922 till 1925 I got odd jobs anywhere I could, but most of the time I was out of work. If I had enough stamps on my card I would get fifteen shillings per week unemployment benefit. If I hadn't, I got nothing.

Chapter Seven

IF we had a shilling, a friend and I would go to a dance. Sometimes I would ask Jo' to lend me Arthur's shoes or his jacket and vest. It was at one of these dances, in 1924, that I met my first wife. We grew very much in love. She had lost her mother and was keeping house for her father and three brothers and was doing a colossal job. I was introduced to her family and duly accepted. They were a wonderful family and in over forty years I have never had a bad word with any one of them: one brother in particular became a close friend and remains so now after all these years.

But I was still out of work and had nothing: not a very good prospect for one who was courting a girl! I used to get home at night and lie awake for hours wondering what the future could hold for me. One night I had a brain-wave. I wrote a letter to the manager of the Labour Exchange telling him my father was going to throw me out as he just could not afford to keep me any longer. Two days after, I signed the register for work and was called into the Manager's office. He told me how sorry he was to think things had come to such a pass at home and that he would make a special effort to try and find me a job.

About a week after, I was called in to see the Manager again. He told me a job was going in Holloway Road making ebony goods, but did I know how to work an oscillated spindle. I said firmly yes that I had had previous experience. He gave me a pretty doubtful look which was fully justified as I had never heard of an oscillated spindle and hadn't a clue as to what it was. However, I stood my ground and was told to go along and was given a green card. I had no money for the fare, so went home and borrowed Arthur's bike. I had the interview for the job and got it. I was told to start next morning and asked how much money I wanted. When I said one and threepence an hour, the Manager nearly fell on his face. After much haggling we settled for one shilling. I was bucked to death to think I had a start at last. I got no sleep that night wondering how I would get on next day. I had to beg and borrow for my fare to Holloway Road. I duly started work and prayed I would master the machine, which I eventually did. I am sure the chaps felt sorry for me and gave me a great deal of help. I didn't get the sack that night, so went home tired but happy. On the Friday night I went to the Labour Exchange to tell them I got the job. The Manager was flabbergasted. He told me the job had been going for three months and they could not find anyone with experience. It just goes to show.

I was now able to help out at home and soon got on my feet. My flat rate was £2 7s. 6d. a week and from August to December there was plenty of overtime. By Christmas I had managed to save enough to rig myself out and to get engaged.

After Christmas 1925, Lydia and I decided we

would like to get married. She was having a tough time of it being housekeeper to four men, and things were not very good at my home. We struggled to save every shilling we could get.

By March 1926 my father's legs began to swell. He was advised to give up drinking, but refused. Mum was worried about him, but there was nothing any of us could do. His whole life had been given to drink and it was too late now.

Lydia and I went ahead with our plans to get married and decided to do so on July 31st, but we could not get a place to live in for love or money. In the last couple of weeks, when we were getting desperate, a friend at work told me his mother had a nice room for rent. Lydia and I went along, saw it and decided to have it on the spot. Our landlady was a delightful person and gave us every help. Meantime, my father had become bedridden. His whole body had swollen to a terrific size, and he seemed to be just waiting to die. But he still had his old drinking pals who came to see him and they would bring him in bottles of beer.

Lydia and I got married and Lydia's people gave us a nice reception. Obviously, the old man couldn't come, neither could my mother as she had to stay with him, but she gave us her blessing which she meant from the bottom of her heart. We soon settled in our new home and were very happy.

Within three months my father died. Mum told us that two nights before he had got one of his pals to sell his trousers and get beer with the money. My mother was left with the princely sum of two farthings, his remaining wealth.

At this point in my life, I end the present narrative, though I hope to continue in a further book of reminiscences, if this book is well received by the public. Mum died in 1946: my sister Jo' in 1947 and my brothers Will and Bert in 1954. Only my other two sisters, Mary and Molly, and myself have survived. Gerry died in 1960, leaving Mary with three fine sons who are rarely out of her company. Molly has one son who is a director of research of one of our greatest Universities. I am still blessed with the love of my wife and that of three good sons who are all making their way in the world. Jo' left one son and two daughters, whom we see frequently and are most kind and considerate to my wife and myself.

So, out of so disastrous a childhood, I am now surrounded, in spite of poor health, with love and happiness—a happiness always denied to my poor mother without whom we should all have either starved or become criminals. Looking back, I still keep asking myself how *she* survived and why she chose to stay with a man like my father. In recent years I have become a believer in the after-life and, if my beliefs are correct, she has found her happiness there. Once through a well-known London medium, my mother told me, speaking of my father, that he was 'more sinned against than he was sinned'; this I have never understood, but perhaps she saw qualities in him or had some knowledge of him that was not evident to us, and this accounted for her loyalty.

Postscript

THESE memoirs first appeared in *Profile*, the magazine of the Hackney Borough Library Services, which enjoys a large circulation in the district where the events it describes took place. Both the library authorities and I were surprised and delighted by the interest it aroused. Many letters were received, not only from the borough itself but from former residents overseas. These letters told of similar memories and similar experiences, so I am satisfied that the picture I have tried to draw was neither exceptional nor one-sided. Talking to middle-class people who did not live in working-class districts, I find that few realise how bad conditions were such a comparatively short time ago. ('Your story reads more like something out of Dickens,' was a typical comment.) It was easy, it seems, for the better-off to be unaware of the appalling poverty and near starvation that existed. But those of us (and there are plenty) who remember lining-up in the snow at the local Mission for a jug of soup or second-hand boots, begging for relief at the Poor Law Institution, being told to take our caps off and address officials as 'sir', realise it all too well. Yet amid those terrible times, we found time to laugh. We did not expect many pleasures out of life, but those we could get we took to the full. Perhaps it was this that enabled *us* to survive and perhaps this is why some of my older readers said they looked back with nostalgia and even affection to some aspects of those old days. To my younger readers, may I say, 'Be thankful that you were born now and not then. Go forward, but try to be tolerant of your parents on the way.'